# William Shakespeare

# Romeo and Juliet

*Edited by*

*John Russell Brown*

The Applause Shakespeare Library
***Romeo and Juliet***

Edited with Commentary by John Russell Brown
General Series Editor: John Russell Brown


***Library of Congress Cataloging-in-Publication Data***

Library of Congress Card Number: 00-111093

***British Library Cataloging-in-Publication Data***
A catalog record for this book is available from the British Library.

ISBN: 1-55783-385-0

**APPLAUSE THEATRE BOOKS**
151 W46th Street, 8th Floor
New York, NY 10036
Phone: (212) 575-9265
FAX: (646) 562-5852
email: info@applausepub.com

COMBINED BOOK SERVICES LTD.
Units I/K, Paddock Wood Distribution Centre
Paddock Wood, Tonbridge, Kent TN 12 6UU
Phone: (44) 01892 837171
Fax: (44) 01892 837272

SALES & DISTRIBUTION, HAL LEONARD CORP.
7777 West Bluemound Road, P.O. Box 13819
Milwaukee, WI 53213
Phone: (414) 774-3630
Fax: (414) 774-3259
email: halinfo@halleonard.com
internet: www.halleonard.com

# *Table of Contents*

*Other Titles in the Applause Shakespeare Library:*

King Lear
Macbeth
A Midsummer Night's Dream
The Tempest
Twelfth Night
Othello
Romeo and Juliet
Antony and Cleopatra
Measure for Measure
Merchant of Venice

# General Preface to the Applause Shakespeare Library

This edition is designed to help readers see and hear the plays in action. It gives an impression of how actors can bring life to the text and shows how certain speeches, movements, or silences take on huge importance once the words have left the page and become part of a performance. It is a theatrical edition, like no other available at this time.

Everyone knows that Shakespeare wrote for performance and not for solitary readers or students in classrooms. Yet the great problem of how to publish the plays so that readers can understand their theatrical life is only beginning to be tackled. Various solutions have been tried. The easiest—and it is an uneasy compromise—is to commission some director or leading actor to write a preface about the play in performance and print that at the beginning of the volume, followed by a critical and historical introduction, the text and notes about verbal difficulties, a textual introduction, and a collation of variant reading as in any other edition. Another easy answer is to supply extensive stage directions to sort out how characters enter or exit and describe any gestures or actions that the text explicitly requires. Both methods give the reader little or no help in realizing the play in performance, moment by moment, as the text is read.

A more thorough-going method is to include some notes about staging and acting among the annotations of meaning, topical references, classical allusions, textual problems, and so forth. The snag here is that the theatrical details make no consecutive sense and cannot deal with the larger issues of the build-up of conflict or atmosphere, the developing impression of character, or the effect of group and individual movement on stage. Such notes offer, at best, intermittent assistance.

In the more expensive one-volume editions, with larger-than-usual formats, yet another method is used to include a stage history of the play showing how other ages have staged the play and describing a few recent productions that have been more than usually successful with the critics. The snag here is that unavailable historical knowledge is required to interpret records of earlier performances. Moreover, the journalistic accounts of productions which are quoted in these histories are liable to emphasize what is unusual in a production rather than the opportunities offered to actors in any production of the play, the text's enduring theatrical vitality. In any case, all this material is kept separate from the rest of the book and not easily consulted during a reading of the text.

The Applause Shakespeare goes further than any of these. It does the usual tasks expected of a responsible, modern edition, but adds a very special feature: a continuous commentary on the text by a professional director or a leading actor that considers the stage life of the play as its action unfolds. It shows what is demanded from the actors—line by line where necessary—and points out what decisions about interpretation have to be made and the consequences of one choice over another. It indicates where emotional climaxes are placed—and where conflicting thoughts in the character's mind create subtextual pressures beneath the words. Visual statements are noted: the effect of groups of figures on stages, of an isolated figure, or of a pair of linked figures in a changing relationship; the effect of delayed or unexpected entries, sudden departures, slow or processional exuents, or a momentarily empty stage. Everything that happens on stage comes within the notice of this commentary. A reader can "feel" what the play would be like in action.

What the commentary does not do is equally important from the reader's point of view. It does not try to provide a single theatrical reading of the text. Rather if offers a range of possibilities, a number of suggestions as to what an actor might do. Performances cannot be confined to a single, unalterable realization: rather, each production is continually discovering new potential in a text, and it is this power of revelation and revaluation that the commentary of the Applause Shakespeare seeks to open up to individual readers. With this text in hand, the play can be produced in the theatre of the mind, creating a performance suitable to the moment and responsive to individual imaginations. As stimulus for such recreations, the commentary sometimes describes the choices that particular actors or directors made in famous productions, showing what effect words or physical performances have achieved. The purpose here is to supplement what a reader might supply from his or her own experience and imagination, and also to suggest ways in which further research might discover more about the text's theatrical life.

The commentary is printed in a wide column on the page facing the text itself, so that reference can be quickly made at any particular point or, alternatively, so that the commentary can be read as its own narrative of the pay in action. Also, to the right of the text are explanations of difficult words, puns, multiple meanings, topical allusions, references to other texts, etc. All of these things will be found in other editions, but here it is readily accessible without the eye having to seek out the foot of the page or notes bunched together at the rear of the volume. The text is modernized in spelling. Both stage directions and punctuation are kept to a minimum—enough to make reading easy, but not so elaborate that readers are prevented from giving life to the text in whatever way they choose. As an aid to reading aloud, speech-prefixes are printed in full and extra space used to set speeches apart from each other; when the text is read silently, each new voice can register clearly. At the rear of the book, an extended note explains the authority for the text and a collation gives details of variant readings and emendations.

In many ways the Applause Shakespeare is a pioneering edition, responding to an old challenge in a new way and trying to break down barriers to understanding that have proved very obstinate for a long time. Further volumes are in preparation and editorial procedures are being kept under review. Reports on the usefulness of the edition, and especially of its theatrical commentary, would be most welcome. Please write to John Russell Brown, c/o Applause Books, 151 West 46th Street, 8th Floor, New York, NY 10036.

# INTRODUCTION

Shakespeare was about thirty years old when he wrote *Romeo and Juliet.* He had completed two tragedies before this: the historical *Richard III* and *Titus Andronicus*, the latter a sensational account of early Rome, replete with pride, envy, murder, intrigue, and rape. In 1595, his next tragedy, *Romeo and Juliet*, appeared. Set in Italy, it is concerned with two young lovers who often speak and act like the characters of his earlier romantic comedies. It is a tragedy that contains laughter, happiness, and sensitivity, however dark and painful its ending. Shakespeare created a strong narrative interest that always keeps an audience keenly involved with what happens next, but at the same time he also explored such issues as the way in which happiness seems fated to turn to suffering in a world that does not understand what love means; how good intentions are not enough; and how the imagination of those in love can make everything else, even death, seem unreal and unimportant—the experience recorded in many of Shakespeare's sonnets:

> But if the while I think on thee, dear friend,
> All losses are restored and sorrows end. (*Sonnet*, xxx)

The imagination of the lovers, their excitement, and their growth in understanding and strength of purpose, are dominant impressions in *Romeo and Juliet.* The two young lovers, from families at war with each other, show, in their meeting, marriage, separation, and deaths, how love is an experience that may lead to "rash" and "unadvised" actions (II.ii. 118), but also

> Courses as swift as thought in every power,
> And gives to every power a double power,
> Above their functions and their offices.
> (*Love's Labour's Lost*, IV.iii.330-32)

Although the story of Romeo and Juliet is apocryphal, the "star-crossed" lovers have so fascinated millions of people since Shakespeare's tragedy was first performed that to this day tourists to Verona, Italy, are shown the house of the Capulets, where Juliet is supposed to have lived, and also Juliet's tomb. A year or two after its first performance, an incomplete and inaccurate text of the play was published and advertised as "it hath been often, with great applause, played publicly." Young Elizabethan men in search of the right things to say to their girls were said to take notebooks to performances of *Romeo* to copy down phrases for their own use. In 1664, when the university library at Oxford sold a copy of the complete works of Shakespeare, the pages containing the scene in which Romeo and Juliet part after their wedding night (III.v) had been thumbed almost to illegibility.

From 1470 onward, the story had already been told by notable Italian, French, and English prose writers, and Shakespeare had found it in a version, written in verse by an Englishman, Arthur Brooke, called *The Tragical History of Romeus and Juliet* (1562). In a world in which marriages were commonly arranged by parents for social and business purposes, sometimes while the bride an bridegroom were still children, the story of two young people who assumed their own right to choose whom they should love, despite the rivalry and hatred of their families, would have had a strong appeal and raised important social issues. Something of the interest of the theme to Elizabethans can be judged by comparing Brooke's preface to the "good Reader" with his comments on the story as he tells it. Introducing his book, he spoke of these "unfortunate lovers, thralling themselves to unhonest desire, neglecting the authority and advice of parents and friends, conferring their principal counsels with drunken gossips and superstitious friars...finally, by all means of unhonest life, hasting to most unhappy death." Yet the cumbersome and careful poem itself alludes to the love of Romeo and Juliet as "perfect," "sound," and "approved," and the friar gives a long and kindly sermon on the ability of reason to triumph over bad fortune. With boldness and sensitivity, Shakespeare tackled the problems that Brooke left unresolved, and his play transcends the particular interests of its own day to kindle our imaginations and alert us to life as we experience it. In the twentieth century, *Romeo and Juliet* has inspired many other works of art. Ballets, operas, and films of *Romeo and Juliet* follow Shakespeare's delineation of character and handling of story, and use, or respond to, his words. Perhaps more than any other of his plays, it has been adapted and modernized, given new settings, styles, forms, and obvious topical relevance, as in the Broadway musical and subsequent film, *West Side Story.*

In telling the story dramatically, Shakespeare often used a wide view, so that his lovers are seen against a background of quarreling and thick-headed servants, street fights, old men reminiscing or giving orders, and other young people dancing, joking, and playing the fool. For the wedding that her father arranges for Juliet, we are shown the musicians turning up for the celebrations only to find that they have to play at a funeral. In the last scene, the tragedy continues for some 140 lines after the deaths of hero and heroine, and in this way Shakespeare is able to show parents, monarch, servants, and the whole cast responding as accomplices, accessories, or observers to the disaster. Such episodes are opportunities for lavish or exciting stage spectacle; yet they are managed so economically that they do not detract from the narrative interest or from the essentially personal and intimate nature of the main theme. In a play of just under 3100 lines of text, more than 270 are spoken as soliloquies. A further 1100 or so—more than one line in every three—are spoken, with only two people on stage. Such a narrow focus is entirely justified by the astonishing vitality of the writing.

In this comparatively early play, there are some scenes in which characters seem to wait to speak in turn, carefully filling out their speeches with relevant and picturesque detail—see for example, I.i.75-153, I.ii.1-44, or I.iv.1-39—but then one or two characters step forward to hold the stage, and at once, between the lines, under the words, in hesitations and odd repetitions, with unlikely epithets, in images that seem to grow one from another, in puns and wordplay that suggest a quickening intelligence and betray excitement, in reported and mimicking speech, and even in moments of complete simplicity or silence, the characters come alive. Words and actions express real and individual personalities immediately engaged in the developing drama. The commentary to this edition repeatedly shows how Shakespeare accomplished this astonishing feat: see, for example, almost every note on what is usually called the Balcony Scene, II.ii.

When first we read the text, the artificiality of Shakespeare's writing will probably occupy our minds. But we must remember that, on the Elizabethan stage, and perhaps more so in Elizabethan life than in our own, "rare" and "brave" words were natural expressions of excitement and uplifted spirits. In *Much Ado About Nothing*, Benedick says that Claudio, his friend, "was wont to speak plain and to the purpose, like an honest man and a soldier," but when he fell in love "he turned orthography; his words are a very fantastical banquet, just so many strange dishes" (II.iii). Romeo is such a lover: meeting Mercutio after he has exchanged vows with Juliet, his verbal wit runs the "wild-goose chase," and he is told, "now art thou what thou art, by art as well as by nature" (II.iv.62-79). In performance, when the actors have mastered the artifice of the writing in this play, it becomes abundantly clear that wit, rhetoric, and poetry all help to express a delighted, energetic, and overflowing response to immediate sensation, and also the force of sorrow, grief, and contrition. The artificiality seems like "nature," as Ben Jonson, his fellow dramatist, characterized Shakespeare's style. George Bernard Shaw said that in Shakespeare's early plays the very verse seems full of a "naive delight," and should be enjoyed by the actors and audience "as an Italian enjoys a barcarolle, or a child a swing" (*Saturday Review*, 2 February, 1895).

When a Broadway production of *Romeo and Juliet*, starring Olivia de Havilland, failed to find favor with the critics in 1951, John Mason Brown blamed neither set, nor casting, nor play, but rather a failure to respond to the poetry:

> Shakespeare's music is more than an asset. It is the play's real business, its excuse and glory, too. Its full, unashamed release is the major source of the mood created and the pleasure given.
>
> (*As They Appear* [1953], p.106)

But this is too simple a statement. The extraordinary achievement of the poetry of *Romeo and Juliet* is that it is true to the action, the physical response, and the inner excitement of the characters, moment by moment. It is not simply music, but theatrical reality as well. The text demands far more from the actors than speech alone: characters "stand…amazed" (Ill.i.128); they touch, sigh and kiss, experience "torture" (III.iii.29); and give themselves over to "blubb'ring and weeping" (III.iii.87); "wanton blood" rushes to their cheeks (II.v.69); and they run out of words, to face each other in understanding silence. A production at the Old Vic Theatre, London, by the Italian director Franco, Zeffirelli was hailed for "unifying words and stage business…making the actors' speech as lively and fluent as their physical action" (*Shakespeare Survey*, 15 (1962), p. 149).

This is the sort of effect that Kenneth Tynan was hailing when he said that Zeffirelli had worked a "miracle":

> The characters were neither larger nor smaller than life; they were precisely life-size, and we watched them living, spontaneously and unpredictably. The director had taken the simple and startling course of treating them as if they were real people in a real situation...It sounds obvious enough; yet the result...is a revelation, even perhaps a revolution...Handled thus realistically, it is sometimes said, Shakespeare's essential quality gets lost. I passionately demur. What gets lost is not Shakespeare but the formal, dehumanized stereotype that we have so often made of him.

To the criticism that lively performance defeats the poetry, Tynan argued that such a view belonged to

> those blinkered zealots who insist that poetry is an arrangement of sounds, instead of an arrangement of words. [In this production] I heard every syllable: meaning and character were wedded, and out of their interaction poetry arose. The production evoked a whole town, a whole riotous manner of living; so abundant and compelling was the life on stage that I could not wait to find out what happened next.
>
> (*Tynan Right and Left* [1967]. pp.49-50)

Each member of an audience and each reader will look for a different mixture of fantasy, formality, excitement, and reality in the play. All are there, and the language and the action can spring alive as the natural idiom of human beings—creatures more gifted, more unfortunate, more passionate than ourselves, but recognizably similar in kind and swayed by the same thoughts, feelings, and instincts as we are.

In choosing as his hero and heroine two young lovers, Shakespeare flouted contemporary notions of tragedy as stories of the rise and fall of kings or as the exposure of vice in high places. Except in the first scene of Act III, he was not much concerned with revenge for honor. In *Richard III* and *Titus Andronicus* he had worked within these preconceptions of what tragedy should be, but, with two inexperienced, private persons at the center of the action, he seemed to follow a medieval notion of tragedy as a tale of prosperity for a time that ends in wretchedness; a tale in which man is viewed as subject to Fortune, or Fate. His lovers are said to be "star-crossed:" at their births they seem to have been doomed to "misadventured piteous overthrows" (Prologue, 6-7). Repeatedly, coincidence and accident seem to govern their fortunes: they meet by accident; by accident, Romeo's intervention in a duel is the immediate cause of the death of his friend Mercutio; by ill-fortune, he arrives at the tomb and kills himself only a few moments before Juliet wakes from the trance that the friar has contrived for her safety. Most noticeable of all such tricks of fate, the friar's letter giving the instructions to Romeo that would have saved both his and Juliet's life was "stayed by accident" (V.iii.251) because the letter's bearer happened to call at a house infected by the plague. As Friar Lawrence, the counselor of both Romeo and Juliet, says in the last scene:

> A greater power than we can contradict
> Hath thwarted our intents. (V.iii.153-4)

This is not to say that everything in the tragedy is predetermined by Fate, so that the main characters do not seem responsible for their actions. Both Romeo and Juliet take their fortunes into their own hands. Romeo is aware that

> Some consequence, yet hanging in the stars,
> Shall bitterly begin his fearful date
> With this night's revels... (I.iv.107-9)

and yet, aware of this, he still chooses to go to the ball where he meets Juliet. She acknowledges by the end of the same night that

> Prodigious birth of love it is to me
> That I must love a loathed enemy. (l.v.138-9)

Yet having given her heart to Romeo, she tells him that she would have it back again:

> But to be frank and give it thee again. (II.ii.131)

They both love freely; both decide to commit themselves to that love before any other human tie. When they see their love as a fate, they accept that fate as their own choice. How they react to misfortune is their own responsibility. In Act III, when Romeo comes from his secret wedding, he finds himself challenged in public by Tybalt, his bride's kinsman: he is to kill Tybalt in a duel, but before he does this he struggles to bring his new values of love to work in the old world of family rivalry. When Romeo is subsequently banished from Verona by the Prince, the friar counsels caution and patience, but the desperation and deep melancholy that cause Romeo to hurry too quickly to Juliet's tomb spring from his own instinctive reactions. Juliet does not take the friar's potion unthinkingly or simply under orders: she is unafraid to drink because she has the inner strength to struggle against the apparition of Tybalt "seeking out" Romeo (IV.iii.56).

The catastrophe that ends the tragedy is not a senseless destruction wrought by blind Fortune. The Prince and the parents alike acknowledge that it is a terrible judgment on an unfeeling world. The lovers hasten events by their own impulsive reactions that are true to their deepest feelings. Having chosen death, they act with new-found self-knowledge and decisiveness, and they find their love kindled by the last acts of union. When the whole company gathers around the dead bodies, it is Providence, not blind Fortune, that the Prince discerns behind the accidents:

> See what a scourge is laid upon your hate,
> That heaven finds means to kill your joys with love.
>
> (V.iii.292-3)

But the chief focus of attention at this time is still the dead bodies of Romeo and Juliet, and these remain onstage as the other characters file off. These corpses represent free, liberating choice, a happiness of the mind or soul that creates its own life and knows no "impediments," that "bears it out even to the edge of doom" (*Sonnet*, cxvi).

As in Shakespeare's later tragedies, other characters beside the protagonists reveal during the course of the action ever deeper qualities, as events test their earlier responses. Juliet's nurse starts as a lovable eccentric, affectionate and loyal to her young mistress, but when Juliet, having already wedded Romeo, is required to marry Paris and asks for advice, the nurse can only counsel more deceit and the acceptance of a second bridegroom. When she supposes Juliet to be dead, she can only cry out repeatedly in horror at the "woeful day" (IV.v.49-54). Mercutio is the liveliest and most fantastic of Romeo's companions. Before he dies from a wound accidentally sustained in a duel with Tybalt, he jests bitterly in a simple and penetrating accusation that reduces Romeo to helpless silence as he hears him out:

> They have made worms' meat of me.
> I have it, and soundly too. Your houses! (III.i.101-2)

In performance, at this last moment, Mercutio can reveal the frustration that has underlaid his energy. Alternatively, Mercutio can say these last words as a gallant jest, as if to exert his wit and attempt to raise laughter in the face of death. Juliet's father and mother, Romeo's father, the Prince, the friar, Juliet's intended husband Paris, the pages, the apothecary who sells Romeo poison, and even Friar John, who carried the vital letter, are all given moments when they make an account of themselves and seem to speak with a deeper truth than previously.

Around the principal roles, a crowd of lesser characters are seen, busy with household festivities, dancing, and fetching food and other necessaries, loitering or fighting in the streets, and facing the incensed judgement of the Prince. Scenes with very little movement, acted as if in moonlight or the first light of dawn, alternate with others of ceremony, riot, restlessness, and the quiet, patient philosophizing of the friar. Repeatedly, the drama changes from lively action with radiant verbal images to fearful action with dark foreboding and a sense of loneliness. The last scene is in a tomb, full of monuments to the dead, recently dead bodies, and the guttering light of torches. A further perspective derives from images of a holy love or the clear light of the sky, intimations of the unmoved reality of the "heavens," the existence of some "greater power" that watches implacably over the efforts of mortals. Besides giving unforgettable images of individual lives and loves in a Renaissance panorama of domestic and city life, the play also indicates further reaches of human aspiration to understanding and peace.

* * *

*Romeo and Juliet* repays strong casting. The most famous production of the present century was in London in 1935, when Peggy Ashcroft played Juliet, Edith Evans the nurse, and Laurence Olivier and John Gielgud alternated the parts of Romeo and Mercutio. Miss Ashcroft had, as the *Times* reported,

> the temperamental sympathy which enables her to preserve the spirit of childhood in the girl who has suddenly become a woman miraculously deep in love. The warmth, the capacity for feeling and for imparting happiness which belong to the woman are beautifully conveyed, but whether ecstatic on the wings of passion or distractedly rushing to death, this Juliet is never far from childhood. (18 October, 1935)

She was a "child who in love, and in nothing but love, is a woman; she has not had time to think, only to feel." Wilson Disher, writing in the *Daily Mail*, saw clearly that when she is so played

> Juliet dominates the action (as distinct from the story), and decides Romeo's fate. Plainly this is what Shakespeare intended, for the new reading gives tense significance to scenes formerly regarded as dull. During Romeo's banishment, Juliet becomes even more vital than when she leans from her balcony in the heartache of romance.

A similar interpretation had already been discovered by Ellen Terry, who had acted with Henry Irving as Romeo in 1882. In her *Lectures on Shakespeare* (1932), she wrote that Shakespeare knew "women have more moral courage than men," and had endowed Juliet, "a very young girl, with the inward freedom which produces this courage." Juliet's recognition that their love is doomed "explains the swiftness of Juliet's surrender, the boldness of her subsequent actions."

According to *The Star* (18 October, 1935), Laurence Olivier's Romeo in the 1935 production added to a gallant bearing "the hot outpouring of words, and the impetuous haste." He was the creature of instinct: "I have seen few sights so moving," wrote the critic for the *Observer*, "as the spectacle of Mr. Olivier's Romeo, stunned with Juliet's beauty, fumbling for words with which to say his love." In contrast, John Gielgud as Romeo substituted "a thoughtfulness that suits the part for an impetuosity that did not" (*Daily Telegraph*), or so thought those critics who remembered that "this supreme tragedy and the Sonnets were written by the same man" (*Times*). Against the "self-absorbed, unselfish eagerness" of Peggy Ashcroft's Juliet, "Mr. Gielgud puts some coldness into his Romeo—as though the tragedy lay in the touching of ice and fire for an instant, and their mutual annihilation. He is Juliet's antithesis. You know that he will destroy her, and that she cannot avoid him."

The subtlety with which Shakespeare's characters can come alive in performance is illustrated in William Hazlitt's account of Miss O'Neill as Juliet in 1814:

> In the silent expression of feeling, we have seldom witnessed any thing finer than her acting, where she is told of Romeo's death, her listening to the Friar's story of the [potion], and her change of manner towards the Nurse, when she advises her to marry Paris. Her delivery of the speeches in the scenes where she laments Romeo's banishment, and anticipates her waking in the tomb, marked the fine play and undulation of natural sensibility, rising and falling with the gusts of passion, and at last worked up into an agony of despair, in which imagination approaches the brink of frenzy... (*The Champion*)

Since the second World War, very different interpretations have become common, especially in the nineteen-seventies and later, when productions have set the play in twentieth-century and not renaissance Italy. Juliet is often a victim today, paying for her innocence, rather than drawing strength from it: her death becomes pathetic rather than a triumph of love. *The Daily Telegraph* noted Sarah-Jane Fenton's Juliet at the Young Vic Theatre in London:

> as a gawky schoolgirl almost overcome by the powerful emotions of first love...The moment when this frail creature, in her trendy teenage clothes, commits suicide in the family vault is deeply affecting. (29 October, 1987)

As with Juliet, Romeo has failed in love because of his own immaturity and the limitations of the society in which he is growing up. In a production of 1990 by Terry Hands for the Royal Shakespeare Company at the Pit Theatre in London, the performances of Mark Rylance and Georgia Slowe made the play:

> less a tale of two great lovers than of two very young people faced with unbearable pressures before they can understand them; two children who—dare one say it?—might even have

> grown out of the love that now seems to them so all absorbing. It is a tragedy of the unformed. (*Times*)

For a German-language production by Karin Beier for the Dusseldorf Schauspielhaus that visited the Barbican Theatre in London in 1994, neither of the actors, Matthias Leja and Caroline Ebner, attempted to show any sustaining power in their love:

> The fact that Leja and Ebner are not transfigured by love is a price worth paying for being able to follow them every inch of the way as two kids who are crazy for each other, and who embark on their forbidden journey like joyriders racing a stolen car. You see them accelerating through the quicksands of desire, showing off, squabbling, and too intoxicated by their new powers to keep an eye on the road. When they come to grief, it was as agents of their own fate, not as victims of a tiresomely contrived plot.

So wrote Irving Wardle in *The Independent* on Sunday 6 November), whereas for Carole Woodis in *What's On*:

> This is very much a Romeo and Juliet defined by its place in a post-modernist youth culture—infantile, headstrong, cynical and respectful of nothing...Caroline Ebner's adolescent but gutsy and ultimately moving Juliet can find little affection...it's little wonder she and Romeo are bound together by a shared immaturity and unawareness of danger. Matthias Leja's Romeo, hopelessly out of his depth as his playful adventure goes terrifyingly out of control, is a young man who never really discovered what life was about. No uplift or catharisis here, only a mournful catalogue of careless blunders and human disasters. Positively chilling.

The production was less a response to Shakespeare's dialogue—it was performed in a very freely adapted German version—than an enactment of the play's action in the light of late twentieth-century ways of living and loving.

Shakespeare's text offers ample scope for individual actors and directors to discover new traits, new strengths and weaknesses: as with the hero and heroine, so for the nurse, Capulet, Paris, and, especially, Mercutio. When Olivier played Mercutio, "never was a man so nearly mad and so well pleased with himself" (*Times*, 29 November, 1935). When Charles Kemble played the role to great applause in the first half of the nineteenth century, "Mercutio's overflow of life, with its keen, restless enjoyment, was embodied with infectious spirit. There was no gall." It was a "noble performance" (W.Marston, *Our Recent Actors* [1896], pp. 80-3). In contrast to both these Mercutios, Alec McCowen played the role "electrically" for Zeffirelli's production in 1960: he was the "unquestioned idol" of the young people of Verona, "an intense, fierce, sourly witty young man, always conscious of his intellectual superiority" (*Tynan Right and Left*, p. 50). In yet another contrast, Colm Feore's Mercutio at Stratford Ontario in 1992 was, according to *Shakespeare Quarterly* (1993):

> always physically loose, whether lolling about over breakfast (spreading himself over table and chair as he did at the start of II.iv) or leaping across the stage on his long, gangly legs or turning costumes, props, and gestures to bawdy purposes.

According to *Shakespeare Survey* (1987) Michael Kitchen's "engagingly drunk Mercutio," in a production by Michael Bogdanov at Stratford-upon-Avon:

> could perhaps be said to have rescued the Queen Mab speech [I.iv.53-94] from the danger of whimsy by speaking it with the fixed scorn of a teenager sending up a soppy bedtime story.

According to *Shakespeare Quarterly* (1996), in a production by Adrian Noble at the same theatre nine years later:

> Michael Lockyer's Mercutio was clearly disturbed. The Queen Mab speech started as exhibitionism and became a dark, unnerving descent into sexual disgust, a dangerous mood from which his friends had to help him recover. He went to Capulet's feast in grotesque drag, with balloons as breasts.

A review in the London *Times*, that called the production a "tragedy of the unformed," wrote of David O'Hara's Mercutio:

> One imagines this pale, uneasy creature transposed to some Glasgow bar [he had assumed a Scottish accent], buttonholing

> the clientele with sexual innuendo, then suddenly, unpredictably clobbering someone with a broken bottle. He is a most unfunny Mercutio, but not untypical of this Verona.
>
> (6 Jan., 1990)

Other characters and other speeches can bear similarly great variations of interpretation, as the commentary to this edition will testify: Capulet, mercenary and unfeeling, or doting, or even guilty of abusing his child; the nurse self-satisfied or truly caring for Juliet; the friar careful and wise or over-confident and meddling; Paris respectfully and ardently in love or conceited and presuming. We have no means of knowing which character traits had most importance in Shakespeare's mind when he wrote the tragedy, or what his first audiences saw in its performance, but at the end of the twentieth century we can see that certain strands in the writing and action can be emphasized to the exclusion of others that had been dominant at the beginning of the century and that the tragedy continues to reflect the interests of new audiences as it was free to do when first written. For readers, too, it is an open text and part of the intention of the commentary to this edition is to draw attention to the possibilities of re-interpretation and new reflections of life.

# *Romeo and Juliet*

## CHARACTERS

CHORUS

ESCALUS, Prince of Verona

PARIS, a young nobleman, kinsman to the Prince Capulet

MONTAGUE, CAPULET, } heads of two feuding houses

AN OLD MAN, of the Capulet family

ROMEO, son of Montague

MERCUTIO, kinsman of the Prince, and friend of Romeo

BENVOLIO, nephew of Montague, and friend of Romeo

FRIAR LAWRENCE, FRIAR JOHN, } Franciscans

TYBALT, nephew of Lady Capulet

BALTHASAR, servant of Romeo

SAMPSON, GREGORY } servants of Capulet

PETER, servant of Capulet, attending on Juliet's nurse

ABRAM, servant of Montague

AN APOTHECARY

THREE MUSICIANS

LADY MONTAGUE, wife of Montague

LADY CAPULET, wife of Capulet

JULIET, daughter of Capulet

NURSE of Juliet

CITIZENS of VERONA, GENTLEMEN and GENTLEWOMEN of both houses, MASKERS, TORCHBEARERS, PAGES, GUARDS, WATCHMEN, SERVANTS, ATTENDANTS.

[SCENE *Verona and Mantua.*]

* an asterisk against a gloss indicates an unusual or new usage

## THE PROLOGUE

[*Enter* CHORUS.]

CHORUS Two households, both alike in dignity,°
In fair Verona where we lay our scene,
From ancient grudge, break to new mutiny,°
Where civil blood° makes civil hands unclean.°
From forth the fatal loins of these two foes,
A pair of star-crossed° lovers take their life;
Whose misadventured° piteous overthrows
Doth with their death bury their parents' strife.
The fearful passage° of their death-marked° love,
And the continuance of their parents' rage,
Which, but their children's end, naught could remove,
Is now the two hours' traffic° of our stage;
The which if you with patient ears attend,
What here shall miss, our° toil shall strive to mend. [*Exit.*]

## Prologue

social rank

violence

blood/passion guilty/befouled (pun: *civil* = decent, refined)

doomed by the stars*

ill-fated*

course doomed to die*

business

i.e, the actors'

**1-14** A single actor takes command of the large stage and speaks as the representative of the actors' company. Because his speech is a formal sonnet, he must deliver it in a measured style, each sentence sustained for at least a separate quatrain; rhyme points specific words; meter is mostly regular, giving prominence to departures from the iambic norm like the reversed feet for "break" and "bury." Moreover, the language demands close attention, with its series of images of warfare, compound words that were new to Elizabethan audiences, and wordplay on "take their life," meaning both to be born and to commit suicide.

The sonnet was popular in sophisticated Elizabethan circles for expressing self-awareness, self-criticism, and witty intelligence. This sonnet-prologue tells the plot of the play and sharpens attention. When the protagonists enter, the audience will have been made aware of the lovers' doom and prepared for a complex response.

# ACT I

Scene i *Enter* SAMPSON *and* GREGORY, *with swords and bucklers,° of the house of Capulet.*

SAMPSON Gregory, on my word,° we'll not carry coals.°

GREGORY No, for then we should be colliers.°

SAMPSON I mean, an° we be in choler,° we'll draw.°

GREGORY Ay, while you live, draw your neck out of a collar.°

SAMPSON I strike quickly being moved.°

GREGORY But thou art not quickly moved° to strike.

SAMPSON A dog of the house of Montague moves me.

GREGORY To move is to stir, and to be valiant is to stand:° therefore if thou art moved, thou run'st away.°

SAMPSON A dog of that house shall move me to stand: I will take the wall of° any man or maid of Montague's.

GREGORY That shows thee a weak slave, for the weakest goes to the wall.°

SAMPSON 'Tis true, and therefore women, being the weaker vessels, are ever thrust to the wall.° Therefore I will push Montague's men from the wall, and thrust his maids to the wall.

GREGORY The quarrel is between our masters and us their men.

SAMPSON 'Tis all one; I will show myself a tyrant: when I have fought with the men, I will be civil° with the maids—I will cut off their heads.

GREGORY The heads of the maids?

small shields

## Scene i

I swear submit to insult

coal dealers / filthy rogues

if enraged draw swords

escape the hangman's noose

made angry

incited

oppose / stand still

(pun on *move,* line 8)

i.e., leave the gutter for

gives way in a struggle (proverbial)

assaulted up against the wall

(obscenely ironic)

**1-38** The contrast could hardly be greater: as the dignified Prologue completes the shapely sonnet, bows and moves offstage, two laughably stupid mutineers take over, brawling between themselves. Both give as good as they get: phrases are mostly short, words emphatically repetitive; each statement is followed by counterstatement; it is a fuss about almost nothing. At line 21 comes the first question, which indicates that Sampson has momentarily outpaced Gregory; it is here that the brutal bragging becomes more explicitly sexual. Actors often accompany the words with illustrative gestures and sometimes chase each other around the stage; if so played, they become wary and still on the entry of the Montagues at lines 28-9.

However, more can be implied in this opening episode: in a Young Vic production (London, 1987), "The endless sexual wordplay, which often seems merely tedious, [was] delivered with offensive vigour, suggesting a mentality in which bully-boy swaggering and the routine degredation of women is the universally accepted norm" (*Daily Telegraph*, 29 Oct.).

Alternatively, the two servingmen can be shown taking their ease, off-duty on a hot day and idly picking quarrels for their own amusement; an audience will sense that this is a casual and usual way of passing the time. Such playing provides an effective contrast when the entry of the rival servants alerts the Capulets and idle amusement turns into lethal agression.

After whispered preparation (ll. 30-8), in which both show some anticipatory fear and probably sheathe their swords (see line 56), Gregory and Sampson step forward together to encounter their enemies.

SAMPSON Ay, the heads of the maids, or their maiden-heads—take it in what sense° thou wilt.

GREGORY They must take it in sense° that feel it.

SAMPSON Me they shall feel while I am able to stand;° and 'tis known I am a pretty piece of flesh.

GREGORY 'Tis well thou art not fish;° if thou hadst, thou hadst been poor-John.° Draw thy tool,° here comes two of the house of Montagues.

*Enter two other servingmen,* [ABRAM *and* BALTHASAR.]

SAMPSON My naked weapon is out: quarrel, I will back thee.°

GREGORY How, turn thy back and run?

SAMPSON Fear me not.°

GREGORY No marry.° I fear thee?

SAMPSON Let us take the law of our sides;° let them begin.

GREGORY I will frown as I pass by, and let them take it as they list.°

SAMPSON Nay, as they dare. I will bite my thumb at them,° which is a disgrace to them if they bear it.

ABRAM Do you bite your thumb at us sir?

SAMPSON I do bite my thumb sir.

ABRAM Do you bite your thumb at us sir?

SAMPSON [*Aside to* GREGORY.] Is the law of our side if I say ay?

GREGORY [*Aside to* SAMPSON.] No.

SAMPSON No sir, I do not bite my thumb at you sir; but I bite my thumb sir.

GREGORY Do you quarrel sir?

ABRAM Quarrel sir? No sir.

SAMPSON But if you do sir, I am for you. I serve as good a man as you.

meaning

feeling

hold my ground/have an erection

i.e., cold-blooded

dried fish sword/penis

back you up

trust me

(a casual oath, from "By the Virgin Mary")

keep on the right side of the law

please

(an obscene gesture, jerking the thumb from the mouth)

**39-56** The Montagues talk less, Balthasar remaining wholly silent; they can, however, provoke the Capulets by their bearing. After Sampson's obscene gesture, Abram directly challenges with deliberate questions. The encounter can be tense: Sampson, who has hitherto taken the lead, draws back warily (l. 42); when Gregory steps forward, Abram withdraws (l. 47).

They quarrel, with noticeably few and simple words, showing brutish stupidity as much as fear. They seem to blunder into stalemate by lines 50-1, but at that point Benvolio's silent entry precipitates the fight by giving extra confidence to the Montagues (l. 55). In a moment swords are out and words give way to fighting.

After an abrupt call, Benevolio's command, expressed in a single and firmly stressed iambic pentmeter (l. 58), can bring about a moment's pause. So played, Tybalt's entry can seem to come exactly on cue and make maximum effect; this is the first of many events that seem to have a fateful timing.

ABRAM No better.

SAMPSON Well sir.

*Enter* BENVOLIO.

GREGORY [*Aside to* SAMPSON.] Say "better"—here comes one of my master's kinsmen.

SAMPSON Yes, better sir.

ABRAM You lie.

SAMPSON Draw if you be men. Gregory, remember thy washing° blow. *They fight.*

BENVOLIO Part, fools!
Put up your swords; you know not what you do.

*Enter* TYBALT.

TYBALT What, art thou drawn among these heartless hinds?°
Turn thee, Benvolio; look upon thy death.

BENVOLIO I do but keep the peace. Put up thy sword,
Or manage° it to part these men with me.

TYBALT What, drawn and talk of peace? I hate the word,
As I hate hell, all Montagues, and thee.
Have at thee coward! [*They fight.*]

*Enter three or four* CITIZENS, *with clubs or partisans.*°

CITIZENS Clubs, bills,° and partisans! Strike! Beat them down!
Down with the Capulets! Down with the Montagues!

*Enter* OLD CAPULET *in his gown,*° and his wife, [LADY CAPULET.]

CAPULET What noise is this? Give me my long sword,° ho!

LADY CAPULET A crutch, a crutch! Why call you for a sword?

CAPULET My sword I say! Old Montague is come,
And flourishes his blade° in spite° of me.

slashing

cowardly louts (sneering pun on fearful deer, *hinds*, without their stags, *harts*)

wield

spears

pikes

dressing gown

(an old-fashioned weapon)

brandishes his sword in defiance

**60-68** For a few moments, Tybalt's entry concentrates attention on his encounter with Benvolio; then, after line 66, many others run on-stage and a full-scale riot breaks out. "In the instant" (see l. 102), the ineffectual quarreling of "fools" (l. 58) is turned to "civil mutiny"; the Prologue had warned of this (l. 3) and so it may seem to be fated. Although Benvolio seeks to "keep the peace," he is soon fighting, as Tybalt threatens him with "death."

Tybalt's aggressive words and rhythms bring a new decisiveness and give a strong impression for the first entry of this character. Benvolio's concern and appeal to Tybalt for help can also make a strong (because contrasting) first impression.

**69-74** As the clamor rapidly increases Capulet and Montague enter, each further complicating the action by struggling against his wife. The stage is now as full as the company presenting the play can manage, reserving only a small but still sizable group of attendants to support the Prince's entry.

*Enter old* MONTAGUE, *and wife,* [LADY MONTAGUE.]

MONTAGUE Thou villain Capulet!—Hold me not, let me go.

LADY MONTAGUE Thou shalt not stir one foot to seek a foe.

*Enter* PRINCE ESCALUS, *with his* TRAIN.

PRINCE Rebellious subjects, enemies to peace,
Profaners of this neighbor-stainèd steel°—
Will they not hear?—What ho, you men, you beasts,
That quench the fire of your pernicious° rage
With purple° fountains issuing from your veins!
On pain of torture, from those bloody hands
Throw your mistempered° weapons to the ground,
And hear the sentence of your movèd° prince.
Three civil brawls bred of an airy word,°
By thee, old Capulet, and Montague,
Have thrice disturbed the quiet of our streets
And made Verona's ancient citizens
Cast by their grave, beseeming° ornaments,
To wield old partisans, in hands as old,
Cank'red° with peace, to part your cank'red° hate.
If ever you disturb our streets again,
Your lives shall pay the forfeit° of the peace.
For this time all the rest depart away.
You, Capulet, shall go along with me;
And Montague, come you this afternoon,
To know our farther pleasure in this case,
To old Freetown, our common° judgment place.
Once more, on pain of death, all men depart.

*Exeunt* [*all but* MONTAGUE, LADY MONTAGUE, *and* BENVOLIO.]

MONTAGUE Who set this ancient quarrel new abroach?°
Speak nephew, were you by when it began?

BENVOLIO Here were the servants of your adversary,
And yours, close° fighting ere I did approach.
I drew to part them; in the instant came
The fiery Tybalt, with his sword prepared;
Which, as he breathed defiance to my ears,

abusers of these swords by staining them with the blood of neighbors

ruinous / wicked

dark red

disorderly / tempered to evil purpose*

angry

some trivial insult

dignified and seemly

rusted through misuse

corrupt, ill-natured

penalty

public

in action

hand-to-hand

**75-97** Often, the Prince is announced with trumpets or drums and supported by superior military strength, but line 77 makes it clear that the fighting does not stop at once. The next lines are usually addressed to those whose "rage" has made them insensible of his authority. By line 82, the last rioter has thrown his weapon to the ground and the crowded stage is impressively quiet.

The speech of the Prince echoes the measured style of the Prologue; often this similarity is accentuated by having one actor play the two roles. The warnings of lines 90-91 and 97 are spoken with the full weight of a royal "sentence," or legal judgment, which threatens torture for everyone and death for the heads of the two warring households, to which the audience's attention will thus be directed particularly (ll. 93-4). As they submit to authority, their followers must silently leave the stage under the watchful eyes of the soldiers in the Prince's "train".

The Prince repeats his order before he leaves the stage (l. 97) which suggests that the crowd has not dispersed readily; its exit can take an appreciable time to enact and stage business can either show the danger and cost of civil mutiny as the wounded are tended or it can give opportunity to suggest continued malice, dissension, or stupidity underlying a pretense of civil peace.

**98-109** The stage is now almost empty and, for the first time, there is no conflict; Montague's questions and Benvolio's considered reply therefore gain close attention. Benvolio's narration is controlled, but he speaks of Tybalt with marked scorn and implies that the riot was inevitable as well as foolish.

He swung about his head and cut the winds,
Who nothing hurt withal,° hissed him in scorn.
While we were interchanging thrusts and blows,
Came more and more, and fought on part and part,°
Till the Prince came, who parted either part.

LADY MONTAGUE O where is Romeo? Saw you him today?
Right glad I am he was not at this fray.

BENVOLIO Madam, an hour before the worshiped sun
Peered forth the golden window of the East,
A troubled mind drew me to walk abroad;
Where, underneath the grove of sycamore°
That westward rooteth from the city side,
So early walking did I see your son.
Towards him I made, but he was ware° of me,
And stole into the covert° of the wood.
I, measuring his affections° by my own,
Which then most sought where most might not be found,°
Being one too many by my weary self,
Pursued my humor, not pursuing his,°
And gladly shunned who° gladly fled from me.

MONTAGUE Many a morning hath he there been seen,
With tears augmenting the fresh morning's dew,
Adding to clouds more clouds with his deep sighs;
But all so soon as the all-cheering sun
Should in the farthest East begin to draw
The shady curtains from Aurora's° bed,
Away from the light steals home my heavy° son,°
And private° in his chamber pens° himself,
Shuts up his windows, locks fair daylight out,
And makes himself an artificial night.
Black and portentous must this humor prove,
Unless good counsel may the cause remove.

BENVOLIO My noble uncle, do you know the cause?

MONTAGUE I neither know it nor can learn of him.

BENVOLIO Have you importuned him by any means?

MONTAGUE Both by myself and many other friends;
But he, his own affections' counselor,

thereby

some on each side

**110-25** Lady Montague's concern for Romeo introduces more personal feeling. While her questions are brief and urgent, the monosyllables of line 111 require careful stressing if they are not to disrupt the imabic norm; their effect is strengthened by a concluding rhyme.

Perhaps Benvolio pauses before replying; certainly his tone has changed. He can speak as if he were half-laughing at Romeo's conventional marks of a melancholy lover; or as if he were truly involved himself—in which case the effect may be comic as he elaborates Romeo's troubles so laboriously. Either way, the complication of verbal style ensures that critical attention is given to this first account of Romeo.

(a tree associated with melancholy lovers)

aware/wary

shelter, cover

feelings

the place where fewest people could be found

followed my whim by not inquiring after his

him who

**125-49** Montague seems to have caught Benvolio's tone: both he and Capulet are capable of sensitive speech when concerned about their only children. Benvolio's questions accentuate Montague's helplessness and his anxiety.

The two couplets (ll. 135-6, 148-9) ensure that the main facts of the situation are clearly understood by the audience, despite all the images and curious elaboration of Montague's descriptions. They also point the dramatic irony of Montague being anxious about Romeo's sorrow and yet unaware of the doom already foretold by the Chorus—the consequence of his own strife and rage.

goddess of the dawn

melancholy (pun on *light*, of weight) (pun on *sun*)

alone confines

Is to himself—I will not say how true—
But to himself so secret and so close,°
So far from sounding° and discovery,
As is the bud bit with an envious° worm
Ere he can spread his sweet leaves to the air,
Or dedicate his beauty to the sun.
Could we but learn from whence his sorrows grow,
We would as willingly give cure as know.

*Enter* Romeo.

Benvolio See where he comes. So please you step aside;
I'll know his grievance° or be much denied.

Montague I would thou wert so happy° by thy stay
To hear true shrift.° Come madam, let's away.
*Exeunt* [Montague *and* Lady Montague.]

Benvolio Good-morrow cousin.

Romeo Is the day so young?

Benvolio But new struck nine.

Romeo Ay me, sad hours seem long.
Was that my father that went hence so fast?

Benvolio It was. What sadness lengthens Romeo's hours?

Romeo Not having that which having makes them short.

Benvolio In love?

Romeo Out . . .

Benvolio Of love?

Romeo Out of her favor where I am in love.

Benvolio Alas that love, so gentle in his view,°
Should be so tyrannous and rough in proof!

Romeo Alas that love, whose view is muffled° still,
Should without eyes , see pathways to his will!°
Where shall we dine? O me, what fray was here?
Yet tell me not, for I have heard it all.
Here's much to do with hate, but more with love.

uncommunicative
inquiry
spiteful

depression, sickness

lucky

confession

**150-53** Couplets speed and accentuate the parents' departures after Benvolio has directed the audience's attention to the silent Romeo who is, in contrast, "so secret and so close" (see line 143).

"Come madam" draws attention to Lady Montague, who has been silent since her questions of lines 110-1; her bearing can suggest deep involvement and sympathy with her son. Perhaps the father's "we" at lines 148 and 149 should refer to her, so making a point of including her in the feelings he expresses.

**154-64** Romeo's answer to Benvolio's cheery greeting can be offhand, abstracted, deeply depressed, or purposefully secretive; or he can be laughably sober. He probably paces about the stage.

As soon as Benvolio speaks of "love," Romeo either hesitates or tries to confuse the issue; the three short lines (160-62) may indicate one or more considerable pauses or else indicate a transition to prose, with each speech spoken in rapid succession. With a return to regular imabics, Romeo reveals the essential truth as he sees it (l. 163); he might blurt this out, impatient with questioning, or emphasize each word as if the facts were almost unbelieveable and quite without justification.

mild in appearance

(Cupid was blindfolded)

desire

**165-76** Romeo's couplet and immediate change of subject (l. 167) suggest that he now seeks to cut off Benvolio's inquiry. So, as he turns away, he sees traces of the "fray," either discarded weapons or bloodstains that lie on the stage. He seems to sympathize instinctively, the clash of love and hate (l.

Why then, O brawling love, O loving hate,
O anything, of nothing first create!°
O heavy lightness, serious vanity,
Misshapen chaos of well-seeming forms,
Feather of lead, bright smoke, cold fire, sick health,
Still-waking° sleep, that is not what it is!
This love feel I, that feel no love in this.
Dost thou not laugh?

BENVOLIO No coz,° I rather weep.

ROMEO Good heart, at what?

BENVOLIO At thy good heart's oppression.

ROMEO Why such is love's transgression.
Griefs of mine own lie heavy in my breast,
Which thou wilt propagate,° to have it prest°
With more of thine. This love that thou hast shown,
Doth add more grief to too much of mine own.
Love is a smoke made with the fume of sighs:
Being purged,° a fire sparkling in lovers' eyes;
Being vexed, a sea nourished with lovers' tears.
What is it else? A madness, most discreet;°
A choking gall° and a preserving sweet.
Farewell my coz.

BENVOLIO Soft,° I will go along.
And if you leave me so, you do me wrong.

ROMEO Tut, I have left myself; I am not here.
This is not Romeo, he's some other where.

BENVOLIO Tell me in sadness,° who is that you love?

ROMEO What, shall I groan° and tell thee?

BENVOLIO Groan? Why no;
But sadly tell me who.

ROMEO Bid a sick man in sadness make his will?
A word ill urged to one that is so ill.
In sadness cousin, I do love a woman.

BENVOLIO I aimed so near when I supposed you loved.

created

169) immediately alerting his mind, so that he speaks with piled-up, sardonic, brutal, and outrageous images. He sees the connection between "brawling love" and the "civil" brawling which has just filled the stage with unnecessary and almost mindless riot. An actor can show surprizing bitterness in this speech, for Romeo is aware, as the audience and Benvolio are not, that Rosaline, whom he loves, is a Capulet (see I.ii.68-9).

constantly awake

Alternatively, Romeo can seem to be merely playing with words, being witty about an obviously dangerous incident in the families' feud in order to minimize its importance. Choice between these two ways of using the speech will do much to mark Romeo as either sensitive or callow before he meets Juliet.

cousin, kinsman

**177-78** Romeo questions Benvolio with heavy irony. His "Good heart" shows, however, that his friend's profession of grief kindles his sympathy, despite the bitterness he feels at Rosaline's rejection.

multiply* oppressed*

**179-288** Romeo retreats from intimacy to talk of himself with such deliberate words (see line 189) that he clouds the issues; he pleads a lover's license not to explain anything or mention any names.

purified (from the smoke)

judicious

bitterness

wait

**189-200** Benvolio pursues Romeo, perhaps chasing him across the stage; this can be funny or very much in earnest. The word "love" again holds Romeo's attention; only, this time, he counters Benvolio's question by mocking his seriousness.

The half-line 195 indicates a pause: perhaps Benvolio has grabbed hold of Romeo; perhaps Romeo delays his reply to tease his friend for his sober persistence.

seriously

(pun: *sad*=sorrowful)

ROMEO A right good markman. And she's fair I love.

BENVOLIO A right fair° mark, fair coz, is soonest hit.

ROMEO Well in that hit° you miss.° She'll not be hit
With Cupid's arrow. She hath Dian's° wit,
And in strong proof° of chastity well armed,°
From Love's weak childish bow she lives uncharmed.
She will not stay° the siege of loving terms,
Nor bide° th' encounter of assailing eyes,
Nor ope her lap to saint-seducing gold.°
O she is rich in beauty; only poor
That, when she dies, with beauty dies her store.°

BENVOLIO Then she hath sworn that she will still° live chaste?

ROMEO She hath, and in that sparing° makes huge waste;
For beauty, starved° with her severity,
Cuts beauty off from all posterity.
She is too fair, too wise, wisely too fair,
To merit bliss by making me despair.°
She hath forsworn to love, and in that vow
Do I live dead, that live to tell it now.°

BENVOLIO Be ruled by me; forget to think of her.

ROMEO O teach me how I should forget to think!

BENVOLIO By giving liberty unto thine eyes.
Examine other beauties.

ROMEO 'Tis the way
To call hers, exquisite, in question more.°
These happy masks that kiss fair ladies' brows,
Being black, puts us in mind they hide the fair.
He that is strucken blind cannot forget
The precious treasure of his eyesight lost.
Show me a mistress that is passing° fair:
What doth her beauty serve, but as a note°
Where I may read who passed that passing fair?
Farewell, thou canst not teach me to forget.

BENVOLIO I'll pay that doctrine,° or else die in debt. *Exeunt.*

plainly seen

retort are mistaken (pun on *miss* a target)

Diana, goddess of the chase

tested strength protected

submit to

endure

(Zeus seduced Danae in a shower of gold)

plenty / offspring

always

thrift / protection of herself

perished

to earn heaven through her conti-nence that makes me sin mor-tally by despair

(proverbial saying: "dead men tell no tales")

to reexamine her delightful beauty(puns: *call in question* = doubt, *exquisite* = beyond question)

surpassing

written account / reminder

carry out my obligation to teach that lesson

**201-19** Benvolio's "hit" can carry a sexual innuendo; if so, Romeo sharply rejects its implication but finds he has been led into thinking of Rosaline. His rhythms become more sustained and for the first time he speaks of her "beauty." His thoughts quicken with a sense of frustration, so that with sharper rhythms he also speaks of death.

At line 212, he answers Benvolio more directly and speaks again of death, tangled with thoughts of happiness and despair. At line 219, Benvolio tries to offer advice; his short, forceful phrases may be accompanied by an attempt to catch hold of his friend.

**220-32** Romeo's "teach me" can be both instinctive and heartfelt, as if Benvolio's efforts to bring him to his senses have, for the moment, succceeded. Benvolio seems to recognize a change for he replies carefully and earnestly, the effect of which is to transfer Romeo's thoughts back again onto ground on which he is sure of himelf in his despair. At once Romeo is able to speak freely again. He starts with a double pun, and then image succeeds image easily. After a less complex pun (l. 230), he simply rejects Benvolio.

The renewed energy and self-confidence of Romeo in his misery can be comic in performance, especially if Benvolio, in speaking his concluding line, has to run after Romeo in order to be heard.

Scene ii *Enter* Capulet, County Paris, *and* [Peter.] *the clown.*

Capulet But Montague is bound° as well as I,
In penalty alike; and 'tis not hard, I think,
For men so old as we to keep the peace.

Paris Of honorable reckoning° are you both,
And pity 'tis you lived at odds so long.
But now my lord, what say you to my suit?°

Capulet But saying o'er° what I have said before:
My child is yet a stranger in the world;
She hath not seen the change of fourteen years.
Let two more summers wither in their pride°
Ere we may think her ripe to be a bride.

Paris Younger than she are happy mothers made.

Capulet And too soon marred are those so early made.
Earth hath swallowed all my hopes° but she;
She is the hopeful lady of my earth.°
But woo her gentle Paris, get her heart;
My will to° her consent is but a part.
And she agreed, within her scope of choice°
Lies my consent and fair according° voice.
This night I hold an old accustomed° feast,
Whereto I have invited many a guest,
Such as I love; and you among the store,°
One more, most welcome, makes my number more.
At my poor house look to behold this night
Earth-treading stars° that make dark heaven° light.
Such comfort as do lusty young men feel,
When well-apparelled° April on the heel
Of limping winter treads, even such delight
Among fresh fennel° buds shall you this night
Inherit° at my house. Hear all, all see;
And like her most whose merit most shall be;

i.e., to keep the peace

repute

request (to marry Juliet)

repeating

prime

## Scene ii

**1-13** As they enter, Capulet is talking soberly and carefully, Paris respectfully—a strong contrast to Romeo with his father in the previous scene. Perhaps there is an air of smug complaceny, for the fray has already become an occasion for compliment and wise sayings.

Paris changes the subject to talk of his own affairs without apology at line 6. He is often played as a spoilt and callow young aristocrat used to having his own way, a representative of Verona's corrupt patriarcy. But his handling of Capulet here and in III.v, together with his consideration for Juliet at all times, do show good sense and some independence of mind.

i.e., children

my chief hope in this world (as opposed to heaven)

in comparison with

among those she favors

agreeing

traditional

plenty

i.e., young girls

i.e., made dark by their absence

i.e., with fresh leaves and flowers

(an herb, with delicate leaves)

enjoy the possession of

**14-33** At lines 14-5, Capulet reflects on his whole life and the death of other children. If the actor takes time, these words can suggest a melancholy that arises out of personal disappointment as well as approaching old age; there can also be a sense of guilt, possibly for a loveless marriage with a bride of fourteen years of age, not old enough to know her own mind. Capulet's apologies at lines 8-12, 24, and 33 and his expressions of pleasure taken in young people provide opportunities for sustaining this suggestion.

Alternatively, lines 14-5 can be said briskly as an excuse for delaying Paris's proposal of marriage. In this case, "gentle" of the next line means noble, rather than kind and considerate, and Capulet will seem intent only on driving a socially advantageous marriage-bargain: his compliments and disclaimers, together with his appreciation of the delicate attractions of unmarried maidens (ll. 28-9), can even sound like the sales talk of a marriage broker.

However spoken, Capulet's long speech gives the actor an opportunity to establish the character. Over-emphasis (accentuated by rhyme) and an insistent personal note suggest a domineering, self-satis-

Which on more view of many, mine, being one,
May stand in number,° though in reck'ning none.
Come go with me. [*To* PETER, *giving him a paper*.] Go sirrah,° trudge about
Through fair Verona: find those persons out
Whose names are written there, and to them say,
My house and welcome on their pleasure stay.°
*Exit* [*with* PARIS.]

PETER Find them out whose names are written here? It is written that the shoemaker should meddle with his yard,° and the tailor with his last,° the fisher with his pencil, and the painter with his nets.° But I am sent to find those persons whose names are here writ, and can never find what names the writing person hath here writ. I must to the learned.—In good time!°

*Enter* BENVOLIO *and* ROMEO.

BENVOLIO Tut man, one fire burns out another's burning;
One pain is less'ned by another's anguish.
Turn giddy, and be holp by backward turning;°
One desperate grief cures with another's languish.
Take thou some new infection° to thy eye,
And the rank poison of the old will die.

ROMEO Your plaintain leaf° is excellent for that.

BENVOLIO For what I pray thee?

ROMEO For your broken° shin.

BENVOLIO Why Romeo, art thou mad?

ROMEO Not mad, but bound more than a madman° is;
Shut up in prison, kept without my food,
Whipped and tormented, and—God-den,° good fellow.

PETER God gi' god'en.° I pray sir, can you read?

ROMEO Ay, mine own fortune° in my misery.

PETER Perhaps you have learned it without book.° But I pray, can you read anything you see?

hold her own

fellow

fied father. Occasional short phrases may indicate a shortness of breath as Capulet exerts his full force. Paris is now silent, and his reserve can accentuate Capulet's energy; it also keeps the audience guessing about Paris's feelings toward Capulet's child, who has still not been named.

wait

measure

mold for shaping shoes

i.e., one should stick to what one knows (but Peter muddles the proberb)

i.e., here comes a learned man

**37-44** At Capulet's departure, which is decisive and brisk, Peter is left standing on stage, alone. He has not said a word yet and, as he blankly repeats his master's words, his bewilderment is comic; and having turned to the audience to complain, so is his attempt to rationalize his predicament.

At this very moment, Romeo enters and so hears of the feast to which he is not invited: yet another fateful coincidence (see commentary on I.i.39-56 and 60-80).

i.e., go forward by going back

i.e., a new love caught through the eye

everyday disinfectant for minor cuts

grazed

(madmen were treated in these ways for restraint and cure)

good evening (afternoon)

**45-57** Benvolio enters as he left the previous scene, still pursuing Romeo. Now he is doing all the talking, more rapidly and in a blunt manner. Romeo says little but sharply mocks his friend's homely truths; probably he is trying to escape from him or to shut him up.

Line 53 suggests that Benvolio has lost patience; however it can be played with genuine concern as if he has not understood what is happening. The incomplete verse-line probably indicates a pause, either before or after he speaks. Romeo's answer has a "mad" energy, which can seem either real or assumed. His list of afflictions stops suddenly in mid-flight as he sees Peter. Perhaps he had become at a loss for more to say and so turned to see Peter gaping at him; or he may have acted as if he were being "whipped and tormented" and so turned round or collided into Peter.

God give you good-evening

(pun: *read* = foretell)

by ear/by heart

**57-62** After Romeo's whirling words, Peter's politeness and simple question (l. 57) are both ludicrous, especially if he has been listening dumbfounded since line 45. He continues to be bewildered, not least by Romeo's self-absorption in "misery" (l. 58). He decides to quit, fearing worse problems.

ROMEO Ay, if I know the letters and the language.

PETER Ye say honestly. Rest you merry.°

ROMEO Stay fellow; I can read. *He reads the letter.*
"Signior Marino, and his wife and daughters; County Anselm, and his beauteous sisters; the lady widow of Vitruvio; Signior Placentio, and his lovely nieces; Mercutio and his brother Valentine; mine uncle Capulet, his wife and daughters; my fair niece Rosaline, and Livia; Signior Valentio and his cousin Tybalt; Lucio and the lively Helena."
A fair assembly. [*Gives back paper.*] Whither should they come?

Peter Up.

ROMEO Whither? To supper?

PETER To our house.

ROMEO Whose house?

PETER My master's.

ROMEO Indeed, I should have asked you that before.

SERVANT Now I'll tell you without asking. My master is the great rich Capulet; and if you be not of the house of Montagues, I pray come and crush° a cup of wine. Rest you merry. [*Exit.*]

BENVOLIO At this same ancient° feast of Capulet's
Sups the fair Rosaline whom thou so loves,
With all the admirèd beauties of Verona.
Go thither, and with unattainted° eye,
Compare her face with some that I shall show,
And I will make thee think thy swan a crow.

ROMEO When the devout religion of mine eye
Maintains such falsehood, then turn tears to fires;
And these who, often drowned, could never die,°
Transparent° heretics, be burnt for liars!
One fairer than my love? The all-seeing sun
Ne'er saw her match since first the world begun.

BENVOLIO Tut, you saw her fair, none else being by:
Herself poised° with herself in either eye.
But in that crystal scales° let there be weighed

God keep you merry

**63-69** Romeo probably betrays his interest in Rosaline by the manner in which he reads her name in contrast with others in the list. Peter usually counts on the fingers of both hands or shows, with some other piece of comic business, that he is trying hard to memorize all the names.

**70-91** Romeo is persistent and patient with Peter, because he is trying to find out about Rosaline. His silence after Peter's exit is marked and can show the depth of his involvement: Benvolio has time to thrust more advice on him.

When he does speak, Romeo is caught up in his own ideas of religious love, tears, fire, and the "all-seeing sun." While denying that anyone could rival Rosaline, he speaks more idealistically than before and finishes with excited exclamation, at which point mockery, impatience, frustration, complaint, and sorrow are all forgotten. He seems to be lost in thoughts of his own purity and of Rosaline's beauty.

In numerous recent productions, however, actors have played this speech against the obvious associations of its high-flown imagery. It can then seem to be an absurd exaggeration, instead of a reverent act of committal and Romeo becomes a comically affected lover at this stage in the play, stupidly and thoughtlessly single-minded instead of strangely other-worldly.

discuss/drink

traditional

Yet another interpretation makes everything Romeo says a boast or an affected pretense, so he makes a mockery of all the feelings and attitudes that he, as a wealthy and eligible young man, is supposed to have.

impartial*

my eyes were often *drowned* in tears, but never went blind

translucent/manifest*

**92-99** Benvolio's dismissive reasoning is quickly answered; again, he is probably left to follow Romeo offstage, or else he goes off in an opposite direction.

balanced

i.e., Romeo's pair of eyes

With the hope of seeing Rosaline, even at his enemies' feast, Romeo is transformed from the brooding, often silent, and quickly sardonic malcon-

Your lady's love against some other maid
That I will show you shining at this feast,
And she shall scant show well that now seems best.

ROMEO I'll go along, no such sight to be shown,
But to rejoice in splendor of mine own.° [*Exeunt.*]

Scene iii *Enter* LADY CAPULET *and* Nurse.

LADY CAPULET Nurse, where's my daughter? Call her forth to me.

Nurse Now by my maidenhead at twelve year old,
I bade her come. What lamb! What ladybird!°
God forbid, where's this girl? What Juliet!

*Enter* JULIET.

JULIET How now, who calls?

NURSE Your mother.

JULIET Madam, I am here. What is your will?

LADY CAPULET This is the matter—Nurse, give leave° awhile;
We must talk in secret. Nurse, come back again,
I have rememb'red me; thou's° hear our counsel.
Thou knowest my daughter's of a pretty age.

NURSE Faith, I can tell her age unto an hour.

LADY CAPULET She's not fourteen.

NURSE I'll lay° fourteen of my teeth—
And yet, to my teen° be it spoken, I have but four—
She's not fourteen. How long is it now
To Lammas-tide?°

LADY CAPULET A fortnight and odd days.

NURSE Even or odd, of all days in the year,
Come Lammas Eve at night shall she be fourteen.
Susan° and she—God rest all Christian souls—
Were of an age.° Well, Susan is with God;

tent of his first entry in I.i.

In productions that stress the fateful nature of the play's action, "I'll go along" is said as if it were a sudden decision that surprises even Romeo. Certainly nothing has prepared the audience for his sudden acquiescence.

i.e., his lady

## Scene iii

**1-12** By introducing the nurse before Juliet, Shakespeare at one stroke made the drama domestic, bawdy, and affectionate in tone. As she speaks in turn to her Lady, to Juliet, and to herself, the nurse's speech is more dynamic and rhythmically varied than any so far in the play. By marking each shade of feeling, an actress can create a lively and idiosyncratic character: Edith Evans's nurse was said to be "earthy as a potato, slow as a carthorse, cunning as a badger" (*Daily Telegraph* [London], 18 Oct. 1935).

sweetheart

By giving so much interest to the nurse, Shakespeare was also able to introduce his heroine almost silently, so that in her first scene Juliet speaks only seven lines. Attention is, of course, focused on her, and her response is crucial for the development of the scene; yet she remains dutiful in speech throughout, and hence mysterious and unknown. Only when her whole being is kindled into life after meeting Romeo does Juliet show in words how intense, far-reaching and delicate is her imagination. Most actresses reveal something of that later energy in this scene, by hints and instinctive physical reactions, perhaps as music is heard at the and of the scene.

leave us alone

thou shalt

In contrast with the nurse, Lady Capulet will appear formal and perhaps coldhearted. After line 1, she usually sits down so that Juliet has to approach her. Her change of mind about the nurse's attendance can make her seem reluctant to speak of marriage to her daughter who is now waiting and listening.

wager

sorrow

August 1

In the Shakespeare Theatre's 1994 modern dress production in Washington, D.C., this whole scene "looked positively homey, for it took place in the kitchen around a table laden with food in preparation for the banquet. The Nurse was sitting at the table shelling peas when Lady Capulet entered, distracted, wearing a glamorous lounging robe and matching turban and waving her freshly manicured nails in the air to dry" (*Shakespeare Quarterly*, 46, 1995).

(her own daughter)

the same age

**12-58** Lady Capulet has asked no question, but

She was too good for me. But as I said,
On Lammas Eve at night shall she be fourteen;
That shall she, marry;° I remember it well.
'Tis since the earthquake now eleven years,
And she was weaned—I never shall forget it—
Of all the days of the year, upon that day;
For I had then laid wormwood° to my dug,
Sitting in the sun under the dovehouse wall;
My lord and you were then at Mantua.—
Nay, I do bear a brain.°—But as I said,
When it did taste the wormwood on the nipple
Of my dug and felt it bitter, pretty fool,
To see it tetchy° and fall out with the dug!
"Shake,"° quoth the dovehouse! 'Twas no need, I trow,°
To bid me trudge.°
And since that time it is eleven years,
For then she could stand high-lone,° —nay, by th' rood,°
She could have run and waddled all about,
For even the day before she broke° her brow,
And then my husband—God be with his soul,
'A° was a merry man—took up the child:
"Yea," quoth he, "dost thou fall upon thy face?
Thou wilt fall backward° when thou hast more wit;°
Wilt thou not, Jule?" And, by my holidam,°
The pretty wretch left crying and said, "Ay."
To see now how a jest shall come about!°
I warrant, an° I should live a thousand years,
I never should forget it. "Wilt thou not, Jule?" quoth he,
And, pretty fool, it stinted,° and said, "Ay."

LADY CAPULET Enough of this; I pray thee, hold thy peace.

NURSE Yes madam. Yet I cannot choose but laugh,
To think it should leave crying, and say "Ay."
And yet I warrant it had upon it° brow
A bump as big as a young cock'rel's stone,°
A perilous° knock; and it cried bitterly.
"Yea," quoth my husband, "fall'st upon thy face?
Thou wilt fall backward when thou comest to age,
"Wilt thou not Jule?" It stinted, and said "Ay."

JULIET And stint thou too, I pray thee Nurse, say I.°

by Mary

(a bitter herb)

can remember

irritable
move (also, sound of earthquake)
I'm sure
be off

quite alone* cross

grazed

he

i.e., for love-making under-standing
holy thing, relic

turn out to be true
if

stopped (crying)

its
testicle
parlous, alarming

(pun: *I* = *Ay*)

the nurse at once assumes the role of informant. She settles to her task, probably sitting down at either line 12 or lines 15-6. The joke against herself (l. 14) brings laughter (at least from herself) and establishes her, for the theatre audience, as an entertainer. The question of lines 15-16 draws her on-stage audience into her reveries about the past.

Although this scene until line 35 has been printed here from the imperfect first Quarto, where it was printed irregularly as prose, the liveliness of the Nurse's long speech is unmistakable and allows the actress to create a dominating and varied performance. The digression about her own dead child (ll. 19-21) can cast a shadow across her more robust feelings. Boasts about a good memory and her realization that she should return to her main tale with "But as I said," invite a self-conscious delivery and suggest the nurse's self-indulgence and comparative forgetfulness about her employer. Juliet is referred to as "she" or "it"; so the speech must be directed to the mother, but most actresses speak it to show that the nurse is also counting on Juliet's avid attention.

The reported words of the nurse's husband together with her memories of the enigmatic "shake" of the dovehouse and the calamitous earthquake, give an immediate, present-tense actuality, especially if spoken with demonstrative mimicry. The bawdy lines 43-5 provide a climax for the speech, making the nurse helpless with laughter and provoking three repetitions, two against the express wish of Lady Capulet. Probably the nurse should make an attempt to be silent or serious and then give in to her own instincts. At lines 53-5, she is still elaborating, as if her mind is still full of joyful and affectionate memories.

**59-66** Juliet's intervention is effective where her mother's (l. 50) was not. She may have been embarrssed by her nurse's bawdiness or may know that more is likely to follow and offend her mother.

The nurse finishes affectionately, speaking now directly to Juliet. The half-line suggests a pause in which she looks at her charge: in many productions,

NURSE Peace, I have done. God mark° thee to His grace!
Thou wast the prettiest babe that e'er I nursed;
An I might live to see thee married once,°
I have my wish.

LADY CAPULET Marry,° that "marry" is the very theme
I came to talk of. Tell me daughter Juliet,
How stands your dispositions° to be married?

JULIET It is an honor that I dream not of.

NURSE An honor! Were not I thine only nurse,
I would say thou hadst sucked wisdom from thy teat.°

LADY CAPULET Well, think of marriage now. Younger than you,
Here in Verona, ladies of esteem,
Are made already mothers. By my count,
I was your mother much upon these years
That you are now a maid.° Thus then in brief:
The valiant Paris seeks you for his love.

NURSE A man, young lady! Lady, such a man
As all the world—why he's a man of wax.°

LADY CAPULET Verona's summer hath not such a flower.

NURSE Nay, he's a flower; in faith, a very flower.

LADY CAPULET What say you? Can you love the gentleman?
This night you shall behold him at our feast.
Read o'er the volume of young Paris' face,
And find delight writ there with beauty's pen;
Examine every married lineament,°
And see how one another lends content;°
And what obscured in this fair volume lies
Find written in the margent° of his eyes.
This precious book of love, this unbound° lover,
To beautify him only lacks a cover.°
The fish lives in the sea, and 'tis much pride
For fair without the fair within to hide.°
That book in many's eyes doth share the glory,
That in gold clasps locks in the golden story;
So shall you share all that he doth possess,
By having him, making yourself no less.

elect

one day

indeed

inclination

(it was thought that vices or vir-tues could be derived through the mother's milk)

at about the same age as you are now, and you are unmarried

model (in wax) of a perfect man

harmonious feature

satisfaction/meaning

margin (where glosses are printed)

without cover/unmarried

binding*/(pun: *cover* = vagina)

as the sea is the element of the fish, so it is fine and proper when a handsome man has the embrace of a beautiful wife

Juliet and the nurse embrace and kiss.

At the Shakespeare Theatre in Washington, D.C., in 1994, "Lady Capulet stood, momentarily forgetting herself, and she gazed affectionately at her daughter and the Nurse with a fond and poignant smile, as though she were remembering events long past. Then she came to herself, recalling her purpose..." and took charge (*Shakespeare Quarterly*, 46, 1995).

**67** Many actresses precede this line with a quick, instinctive, and nonverbal reaction, so emphasizing the composed and respectful tone of the words and marking the restraint with which Juliet speaks to her mother. Alternatively, the line can be said with simple and disarming truth, suggesting a serious mind and an intense idealism.

**70-80** Juliet's silence draws attention to her, especially after her mother's two unanswered questions at line 80.

The nurse now becomes comparatively speechless, wholly forgetting herself in excitement about Juliet. She may hug or kiss Juliet, or gaze at her as if she were the subject of her praise (ll. 76-7). At lines 78 and 80, Lady Capulet may have to break in on an unspoken mutual confidence between the nurse and Juliet. However, Juliet may be lost in her own, separate daydream. At line 80, Lady Capulet has to insist on getting some positive response.

**81-95** The allusions grow more and more sexual, as if Lady Capulet wishes to heighten Juliet's expectation without speaking directly of the experience of marriage. An actress can here suggest reserve, distaste, or cunning: some such hidden motivation seems almost obligatory to sustain the ingenuity and extent of the simile with which Lady Capulet holds attention and the emphases given by rhyme and repetition.

NURSE No less ? Nay, bigger! Women grow° by men.

LADY CAPULET Speak briefly, can you like of Paris' love?

JULIET I'll look° to like, if looking liking move.
But no more deep will I endart mine eye
Than your consent gives strength to make it fly.

*Enter* SERVINGMAN.

SERVINGMAN Madam, the guests are come, supper served up, you called, my young lady asked for, the Nurse cursed in the pantry, and everything in extremity. I must hence to wait;° I beseech you follow straight.° [*Exit.*]

LADY CAPULET We follow thee. Juliet, the county stays.°

NURSE Go girl, seek happy nights to happy days. *Exeunt.*

Scene iv *Enter* ROMEO, MERCUTIO, BENVOLIO, *with five or six other* MASKERS; TORCHBEARERS.

ROMEO What, shall this speech be spoke for our excuse?°
Or shall we on without apology?

BENVOLIO The date is out of such prolixity.°
We'll have no Cupid, hoodwink'd° with a scarf,
Bearing a Tartar's painted bow of lath,
Scaring the ladies like a crowkeeper;°
Nor no without-book° prologue, faintly spoke
After the prompter, for our entrance.
But let them measure° us by what they will,
We'll measure° them a measure,° and be gone.

ROMEO Give me a torch. I am not for this ambling;
Being but heavy,° I will bear the light.°

MERCUTIO Nay gentle Romeo, we must have you dance.

ROMEO Not I, believe me. You have dancing shoes
With nimble soles; I have a soul of lead
So stakes° me to the ground I cannot move.

are made pregnant

**97-100** When at last Juliet responds, she is conventional and modest; her restraint is obvious, but there is also power in the rhymes and in images like "deep," "endart," and "fly"; the neat wordplay of line 98 suggests a quick intelligence.

expect (pun on *looking*=looking at him)

**101-6** Usually, the servant is Peter who was in the previous scene. His rapid catalogue of extremities and his rapid exit quicken the tempo. Often, he speaks from the doorway, barely giving himself time to come on-stage. In strong contrast, Juliet stands silent as both mother and nurse summon her to the feast. Lady Capulet usually walks off as she speaks, so that the nurse has a moment of free speech to Juliet.

serve

immediately

is waiting

"Go" of the last line suggests that the nurse waits to be the last to leave. Juliet sometimes kisses the nurse, or dances on ahead, or walks as if playing the "lady"; the focus is almost wholly on her at this moment.

In Karin Beier's modern dress production of 1994 (see Introduction, p. xix), Lady Capulet "thrust" Juliet into adulthood: she "gives her a pair of high-heeled shoes; she joyfully tries them on, has difficulty balancing but is denied her old ones. There is no going back from marriage" (*Times* [London], 1 Nov.)

## Scene iv

(for breaking into the feast as maskers)

**1-18** The stage suddenly fills with lights and grotesquely disguised figures. There may be whispering, quiet laughter, and a drumbeat (see line 114) or other music; there is a sense of expectant preparation and nighttime excitement. Romeo's speeches are out of key with the mood of all others on-stage.

such wordiness is out of fashion

blindfolded

Benvolio speaks with unaccustomed energy and some editors suppose that lines 3-10 were intended for Mercutio. Such a change would lose the dramatic effect of Mercutio's delayed emergence from the crowd with a decisive first line that clearly opposes him to Romeo while suggesting warm friendship and admiration. On line 13 or 18, some Mercutios start to dance, drawing Romeo to go with him.

scarecrow

memorized

judge

tread dance

melancholy (puns on *light* = cheerful, and light in weight)

fastens*

MERCUTIO You are a lover: borrow Cupid's wings,
And soar with them above a common bound.°

ROMEO I am too sore enpiercèd with his shaft
To soar with his light feathers; and so bound,
I cannot bound a pitch° above dull° woe.
Under love's heavy burden do I sink.

MERCUTIO And to sink in it should you burden love:°
Too great oppression for a tender thing.

ROMEO Is love a tender thing? It is too rough,
Too rude, too boist'rous, and it pricks° like thorn.

MERCUTIO If love be rough with you, be rough with love;
Prick love for pricking,° and you beat love down.
Give me a case° to put my visage in.
A visor° for a visor! What care I
What curious eye doth quote° deformities?
Here are the beetle brows° shall blush for me.

BENVOLIO Come, knock and enter; and no sooner in
But every man betake him to his legs.°

ROMEO A torch for me! Let wantons light of heart
Tickle the senseless rushes° with their heels,
For I am proverbed with a grandsire phrase:°—
I'll be a candleholder,° and look on;
The game was ne'er so fair, and I am done.°

MERCUTIO Tut! Dun's the mouse,° the constable's own word!
If thou art Dun,° we'll draw thee from the mire
Of—save your reverence°—love, wherein thou stickest
Up to the ears. Come, we burn daylight,° ho!

ROMEO Nay, that's not so.

MERCUTIO I mean, sir, in delay
We waste our lights° in vain, like lights by day.
Take our good meaning,° for our judgment sits
Five times in that, ere once in our five wits.°

ROMEO And we mean well in going to this masque;
But 'tis no wit° to go.

MERCUTIO Why, may one ask?

limit/leap

height heavy/stupid

you must lie on your love, to lose yourself in lovemaking

hurts

being aroused (sexual pun)

i.e., mask

mask

observe

i.e., the ugly mask

begin dancing

(used as floor covering)

old man's saying

one who only sees the game* (proverb: leave when game is at its best)

be quiet

(horse's name; pun on *done*, line 39)

with apologies

waste time

perceptions/torches

intention

senses

(wordplay on *wits*, line 47)

**19-43** By this time, all the maskers are watching Mercutio's verbal duel with Romeo and will respond as points are scored on each side. Sexual innuendoes become progressively more blatant until, after line 28, Mercutio assumes that he has won the contest and calls for a mask in preparation for departure. However lines 30-2 are strangely ambiguous, either alluding to his own ugliness or suggesting that all their entertainment will be harsh and brutal.

When Romeo again asks to be only a torchbearer, Mercutio mocks him more broadly and promises to "draw" him into the party.

Although Mercutio implies that Romeo is a dullard (l. 41) and, perhaps, that he has been blushing (l. 32), Romeo holds his own, calling for a torch with increased spirit (compare lines 11 with 35) and mocking both his friends and himself. He knows (as does Benvolio) that he goes to see Rosaline and so does not wish to be drawn in to become one of a boisterous gang.

**44-49** Romeo now resists Mercutio by taking pedantic exception to his wit; his friend, with mocking politeness, dutifully explains. Then something happens to Romeo, for he suddenly says it is unwise to go. With mock respect, Mercutio bluntly asks the reason.

ROMEO I dreamt a dream tonight.°

MERCUTIO And so did I.

ROMEO Well, what was yours?

MERCUTIO That dreamers often lie.

ROMEO In bed asleep, while they do dream things true.

MERCUTIO O then I see Queen Mab hath been with you.
She is the fairies' midwife,° and she comes
In shape no bigger than an agate° stone
On the forefinger of an alderman,
Drawn with a team of little atomies°
Over men's noses as they lie asleep;
Her wagon spokes made of long spinners'° legs;
The cover,° of the wings of grasshoppers;
Her traces,° of the smallest spider web;
Her collars, of the moonshine's wat'ry beams;
Her whip, of cricket's bone; the lash, of film;°
Her wagoner, a small gray-coated gnat,
Not half so big as a round little worm
Pricked from the lazy finger of a maid.°
Her chariot is an empty hazelnut,
Made by the joiner squirrel or old grub,°
Time out o' mind the fairies' coachmakers.
And in this state° she gallops night by night
Through lovers' brains, and then they dream of love;
O'er courtiers' knees, that dream on curtsies° straight;
O'er lawyers' fingers, who straight dream on fees;
O'er ladies' lips, who straight on kisses dream,
Which oft the angry Mab with blisters plagues,
Because their breath with sweetmeats tainted are.
Sometime she gallops o'er a courtier's nose,
And then dreams he of smelling out a suit;°
And sometime comes she with a tithe° pig's tail,
Tickling a parson's nose as 'a lies asleep,
Then he dreams of another benefice.
Sometime she driveth o'er a soldier's neck,
And then dreams he of cutting foreign throats,
Of breaches, ambuscadoes,° Spanish blades,°
Of healths five fathom deep;° and then anon

last night

**50-51** With everyone else ready to leave the stage, with music, torches, and general excitement, Romeo strikes a new note, expressing something of an irrational foreboding that must have been in his mind during the whole of the scene. When Mercutio flippantly echoes him, Romeo again masks his deepest feelings and encourages Mercutio to do the talking. Something in these two lines touch a spring that releases Mercutio's fantasy at once; it can be either affection for Romeo, or rivalry or, even, fear of him. Romeo keeps his feelings to himself, at least until his last speech in the scene.

i.e., she helps give birth to men's fantasies

(on a signet ring)

tiny creatures

**53-71** As if sensing that Romeo is indeed troubled, Mercutio forgets leaving to go to the mask. As he gives rein to his fantasies, he gains attention at once; the maskers hold back to listen, either with jeers, that are also a form of applause, or in rapt silence.

long-legged spiders

wagon hood

part of the harness

Most Mercutios speak lightly and precisely as they list the minute accouterments of Queen Mab. There is perhaps a self-imposed contest in setting out to complete the delicate catalogue. Mercutio's success may be applauded as he rounds off with lines 70-1 and ends triumphantly with "love." This in turn leads to another list, this time of the Queen's victims.

filament, gossamer

(maggots were said to breed in the fingers of lazy maids)

(squirrels gnaw nuts, and grubs bore holes in them)

royal array

**72-95** This list offers the actor the opportunity to mimic in voice and action each one of the sleepers visited by Queen Mab: so, for example, he will use a nasal, pious voice for the avaricious parson, a loud, bragging manner and alarming action for the soldier. His stage audience will respond as Mercutio grows in confidence and in pleasure at his own outrageous fantasies. He is an entertainer at ease with his audience, improvising with dazzling precision and variety. He becomes more mysterious and then, quite quickly, more bawdy (in some phrases echoing the nurse's report of her husband's joke).

bows

petition

tenth (part of the parson's tithe or dues)

This "Queen Mab speech" is the actor's opportunity to establish the character of Mercutio. It can suggest the quickness, sensuality, and aggressive nature of his imagination, and the finesse, range, and destructive nature of his intelligence. Above all, he is seen as ringleader around whom the whole party gathers and will wait despite their eagerness to get to the ball. He is also a contestant who at once takes up Romeo's challenge. The speech can be spoken as

ambushes swords

deep drinking

Drums in his ear, at which he starts and wakes,
And being thus frighted, swears a prayer or two°
And sleeps again. This is that very Mab
That plats the manes of horses in the night,
And bakes° the elflocks° in foul sluttish hairs,
Which once untangled much misfortune bodes.
This is the hag,° when maids lie on their backs,
That presses them and learns them first to bear,
Making them women of good carriage.°
This is she—

ROMEO Peace, peace, Mercutio, peace!
Thou talkst of nothing.

MERCUTIO True, I talk of dreams;
Which are the children of an idle brain,
Begot of nothing but vain° fantasy;
Which is as thin of substance as the air,
And more inconstant than the wind, who woos
Even now the frozen bosom of the North
And, being angered, puffs away from thence,
Turning his side to the dew-dropping South.

BENVOLIO This wind you talk of blows us from ourselves:
Supper is done, and we shall come too late.

ROMEO I fear, too early: for my mind misgives
Some consequence, yet hanging in the stars,
Shall bitterly begin his° fearful date°
With this night's revels, and expire° the term
Of a despisèd life closed in my breast
By some vile forfeit of untimely death.
But he that hath the steerage° of my course
Direct my sail! On, lusty gentlemen!

BENVOLIO Strike, drum. *They march about the stage.*

(to ward off evil)

cakes tangles

evil, malicious spirit

posture/ability to bear children

worthless

its duration

conclude (*life* being spoken of as a legal contract or bond)

direction

an improvised divertissement: which Charles Kemble made "apparently as fresh to himself as to the listener:" he "abandoned himself to the brilliant and thronging illustrations which, amidst all their rapidity and fire, never lost the simple and spontaneous grace of nature in which they took rise. Mercutio's overflow of life, with its keen, restless enjoyment, was embodied with infectious spirit" (W. Marston, *Our Recent Actors* [1890], pp. 80-1). While this nineteenth-century actor made a wholly attractive character of Mercutio, many actors today will show bitterness, aggression, and frustration in these impulsive fantasies, as in both stage and film versions directed by Franco Zeffirelli in the 1960s. See, also, Introduction, pp. xxi.

At line 95, Romeo may sense that Mercutio is about to deal with his fantasies of love and sex (he may now be pointed at), and so he interrupts.

**96-103** Mercutio changes key at once. Some actors reply sharply at first with "True!" and then continue more slowly with "I talk of dreams." Now Mercutio can speak quite coolly, looking at Romeo. What he says, in effect, is: "Why bother with your dreams of 'frozen' love when there is the warmth of the south? And why dream at all?" But his imagery and rhythms are not without sensitivity. To this, Romeo has no reply.

**104-14** Benvolio hustles the others on, but Romeo stays unmoving and unmoved. His simple, unexpected contradiction, "I fear, too early," may slip from him involuntarily. Then, despite his earlier reticence, he is drawn on to explain. A single sustained sentence that ends with "death" is the most depressed and doomed speech in his part so far; it will hold attention in contrast to the renewed and light-hearted activity of everyone else on stage, so accentuating its deeply-rooted foreboding.

When, at lines 112-3, Romeo decides to go, it can seem like an involuntary, wholly unexpected act, a freak of the fate announced in the play's prologue. Suddenly he is at one with the "lusty gentlemen." The drum strikes up, and the whole party is noisily in progress.

In the Shakespeare Theatre's 1994 production in Washington, D.C., Romeo's friends "stood awkwardly about, looking at him with confusion; Mercutio then crossed the stage and embraced him warmly, pulling back to hold him by the shoulders and gaze at him with love and concern. Romeo's decision to go forward became an act of reassurance to Mercutio" (*Shakespeare Quarterly*, 46).

Scene v SERVINGMEN *come forth with napkins.*

FIRST SERVINGMAN Where's Potpan, that he helps not to take away? He shift a trencher?° He scrape a trencher?

SECOND SERVINGMAN When good manners shall lie all in one or two men's hands and they unwashed too, 'tis a foul° thing.

FIRST SERVINGMAN Away with the join-stools,° remove the court cupboard,° look to the plate.° Good thou, save me a piece of marchpane;° and as thou loves me, let the porter let in Susan Grindstone and Nell. Antony, and Potpan!

THIRD SERVINGMAN Ay boy, ready.

FIRST SERVINGMAN You are looked for and called for, asked for and sought for, in the great chamber.°

FOURTH SERVINGMAN We cannot be here and there too. Cheerly boys! Be brisk awhile, and the longer liver take all.°

*Exeunt* [SERVINGMEN.]

*Enter* CAPULET, LADY CAPULET, JULIET, TYBALT, NURSE, *and all the* GUESTS *and* GENTLEWOMEN *to the Maskers.*

CAPULET Welcome gentlemen! Ladies that have their toes
Unplagued with corns will walk a bout° with you.
Ah ha! my mistresses, which of you all
Will now deny° to dance? She that makes dainty,°
She I'll swear hath corns. Am I come near ye° now?
Welcome gentlemen! I have seen the day
That I have worn a visor and could tell
A whispering tale in a fair lady's ear,
Such as would please. 'Tis gone, 'tis gone, 'tis gone.
You are welcome, gentlemen. Come musicians, play.

*Music plays, and they dance.*

A hall,° a hall! Give room, and foot it, girls!
More light you knaves, and turn the tables up;°

Scene v

wooden plate

dirty / unfair

stools made by carpenter

sideboard tableware

marzipan (a desert)

main living room

take the jackpot (proverb implying that nothing matters when you are dead)

**1-13** As the maskers march around the stage, so representing their journey to Capulet's house, the lively stage picture and drumming are augmented by two servants; they are called "boys" in the text, rather than "sevingmen" as in the stage direction. They run on-stage complaining, and then shouting orders and calling out for others (ll. 5-8); they then meet and dispatch two more servants.

The first of these servingmen dominates, with short, emphatic, repetitive phrases, the rhythms varied only when he looks after his own appetite for marchpane and makes sure Susan and Nell come to the feast. They all run off or come to silent attention as Capulet enters with the procession of his guests. When he greets the maskers, the dances can begin.

There is scope for many formal ceremonies before the maskers appear. At Stratford, Ontario, in 1992, "The ball provided a glimpse of a powerful, wealthy, and patriarchal system in operation when Juliet, entering above to the applause of all the characters onstage, descended to her mother, who passed her on to Capulet for a dance, who then relayed her to Paris" (*Shakespeare Quarterly*, 44, 1993).

contest / round, set

refuse holds back

have I found you out

**14-26** Capulet's busily assertive talk increases expectation and hurries the arrangements for the dance. The maskers are an unplanned addition to the annual feast and their strange and, probably, ugly masks may well intimidate Capulet's guests and so necessitate the host's encouraging (and boastful) badinage.

The muddled reminiscences of the two older men, sitting apart from the festivities, are a foil to Romeo's question (ll. 39-40), which is alive with both immediate concern and fanciful imagery.

clear the floor*

dismantle and upend the tables

And quench the fire, the room is grown too hot.
Ah sirrah, this unlooked-for sport° comes well.
Nay sit, nay sit, good cousin° Capulet,
For you and I are past our dancing days.
How long is't now since last yourself and I
Were in° a mask?

SECOND CAPULET By'r lady, thirty years.

CAPULET What man, 'tis not so much, 'tis not so much.
'Tis since the nuptial of Lucentio,
Come Pentecost as quickly as it will,
Some five-and-twenty years, and then we masked.

SECOND CAPULET 'Tis more, 'tis more. His son is elder sir;
His son is thirty.

CAPULET Will you tell me that?
His son was but a ward° two years ago.

ROMEO [*To a* SERVINGMAN.] What lady's that which doth enrich the hand
Of yonder knight?

SERVINGMAN I know not sir.

ROMEO O, she doth teach° the torches to burn bright!
It seems she hangs upon the cheek of night
Like a rich jewel in an Ethiop's ear:
Beauty too rich for use,° for earth° too dear!°
So shows° a snowy dove trooping with crows,
As yonder lady o'er her fellows shows.
The measure° done, I'll watch her place of stand
And, touching hers, make blessèd my rude° hand.
Did my heart love till now? Forswear° it, sight;
For I ne'er saw true beauty till this night.

TYBALT This, by his voice,° should be a Montague.
Fetch me my rapier, boy. What dares the slave
Come hither, covered with an antic face,°
To fleer and scorn° at our solemnity?°
Now by the stock and honour of my kin,
To strike him dead I hold it not a sin.

CAPULET Why how now, kinsman, wherefore storm you so?

i.e., the unexpected maskers
kinsman

wore

minor

(because she outshines them)

everyday usage life/grave beloved/costly
appears

dance
simple, rough (earthly, not divine)
deny with oath

(Romeo is masked)

grotesque mask
sneer and mock celebration

**27-40** Center-stage is now occupied by the dancing couples. Romeo stands aside, perhaps moving around so that he can look for Rosaline (and so see Juliet) and, incidentally, be noticed by the audience. The torch he carries will also help to draw attention to him.

Formal dances of the period were mostly dignified and slow, but the maskers would encourage livelier dancing than usual and also some excitement of the unknown.

**41-51** The servant's response is unexpected, since he should be able to recognize the daughter of the house in which he lives; perhaps he is too busy with some duty to give proper attention or, perhaps, Romeo's "enrich" confuses him. The incomplete verse-line indicates that he pauses before answering Romeo's question. Romeo's next line, with its new sense of wonder and involvement, is a total contrast that will catch the audience's attention; it pays no attention to the unhelpful answer.

Romeo's imagery becomes more complex and exalted; his rhythms lengthen, and each line is pointed with rhyme, the first reaching back to "knight" (line 40) and forward to "night." Characteristically, darkness comes into his thoughts at the very moment that he sees this new and amazing "light."

At some point, Romeo puts down or passes on the torch he has carried; this business will help to draw attention to him and his new purpose. He is still disguised as a masker (see line 54).

**52-80** Tybalt steps out of the dance or from the concourse of onlookers. He speaks decisively and in fully-controlled sentences: the effect is of dangerous

TYBALT Uncle, this is a Montague, our foe:
A villain that is hither come in spite,
To scorn at our solemnity this night.

CAPULET Young Romeo is it?

TYBALT 'Tis he, that villain Romeo.

CAPULET Content thee, gentle coz,° let him alone.
'A bears him like a portly° gentleman:
And to say truth, Verona brags of him
To be a virtuous and well-governed youth.
I would not for the wealth of all this town
Here in my house do him disparagement.°
Therefore be patient; take no note of him.
It is my will, the which if thou respect,
Show a fair presence, and put off these frowns,
And ill-beseeming semblance° for a feast.

TYBALT It fits when such a villain is a guest.
I'll not endure him.

CAPULET He shall be endured.
What, goodman° boy! I say he shall. Go to!°
Am I the master here, or you? Go to!
You'll not endure him! God shall mend my soul,
You'll make a mutiny° among my guests!
You will set cock-a-hoop!° You'll be the man!°

TYBALT Why, uncle, 'tis a shame.

CAPULET Go to, go to!
You are a saucy° boy. Is't so indeed?
This trick° may chance to scathe° you. I know what:°
You must contrary me! Marry, 'tis time—
Well said, my hearts!°—You are a princox,° go!
Be quiet, or—More light, more light!—For shame!
I'll make you quiet. What!—Cheerly, my hearts!

TYBALT Patience perforce° with willful choler° meeting
Makes my flesh tremble in° their different° greeting.
I will withdraw; but this intrusion shall,
Now seeming sweet, convert to bitt'rest gall. *Exit.*

ROMEO If I profane with my unworthiest hand

and disruptive power (see l. 58).

Mercutio's nickname for him, "King of Cats" (III.i.73; Tybalt was the cat's name in medieval Reynard the Fox fables) is often taken by actors as a cue to give Tybalt a physical bearing that is proud and finely strong, capable of rapid precise action. So his simple words at lines 62 and 74 are not petulant but sharp and unreflective, like an arrow striking center target.

cousin

proper, dignified

Capulet probably goes over to Tybalt at line 58, but Tybalt may cross the stage and speak lines 52-7 to him, rather than in soliloquy or to the audience. Capulet's conscious good sense at first contrasts with Tybalt's hostility. At line 74, however, he becomes more urgent; his phrasing is short, repetitive, and sarcastic. He probably draws Tybalt further apart and has to struggle, perhaps unsuccessfully, to keep his own voice quiet and his anger and, possibly his fear, under control.

dishonor him

The dance continues during this duologue. Although Romeo may have moved to be closer to Juliet, Tybalt will continue to keep his eyes (and so the audience's) fixed on him.

appearance giving a wrong/bad impression

i.e., you are not a gentleman enough (implying impatience and derision)

disturbance

give way to riot (derisive)

**81-90** Tybalt probably receives his sword from his attendant just before "Is't so indeed?" (l. 81). The dance ends after line 83 and Capulet must then attempt to look after his guests while continuing to pacify Tybalt.

insolent

carrying-on, behavior

injure what's what

friends (the guests)

upstart

Tybalt now either has lost sight of Romeo or finds himself attracting unwanted attention; either way, he must now withdraw. Lines 87-8 could imply that he has physically come to breaking point and is so enraged and frustrated that he recognizes the need for postponing his revenge for a less public occasion. Although the stage is busy with activity as attendants bring on "more light" and a new dance starts, the decisive rhymes will help Tybalt to hold the focus of attention until he has left the stage.

enforced patience anger of my will

shake with opposed

**91-104** Because of the attention gained by Tybalt,

This holy shrine, the gentle sin is this:°
My lips, two blushing pilgrims, ready stand
To smooth that rough touch with a tender kiss.

JULIET Good pilgrim, you do wrong your hand too much,
Which mannerly° devotion shows in this;
For saints have hands that pilgrims' hands do touch,
And palm to palm is holy palmers'° kiss.

ROMEO Have not saints lips, and holy palmers too?

JULIET Ay pilgrim, lips that they must use in prayer.

ROMEO O then, dear saint, let lips do what hands do!
They pray;° grant thou, lest faith turn to despair.

JULIET Saints do not move,° though grant for prayers' sake.

ROMEO Then move not°, while my prayer's effect I take.
[*Kisses her.*]
Thus from my lips, by thine my sin is purged.

JULIET Then have my lips the sin that they have took.

ROMEO Sin from thy lips? O trespass sweetly urged!
Give me my sin again.

JULIET You kiss by th' book.° [*They kiss.*]

NURSE Madam, your mother craves a word with you.

ROMEO What is her mother?

NURSE Marry, bachelor,
Her mother is the lady of the house,
And a good lady, and a wise and virtuous.
I nursed her daughter that you talked withal.°
I tell you, he that can lay hold of her
Shall have the chinks.°

ROMEO Is she a Capulet?
O dear° account:° my life is my foe's debt!°

BENVOLIO Away, be gone; the sport is at the best.°

ROMEO Ay, so I fear; the more is my unrest.

CAPULET Nay gentlemen, prepare not to be gone;
We have a trifling foolish banquet° towards.°

mild/courteous sin is in this

seemly

pilgrims from Holy Land, carrying palm leafs

lips pray that they may kiss

urge/take the lead

be still

according to rule

with

money

fateful/costly reckoning  statement/ my foe now owns my life (see I.iv.39)

refreshments  ready

the audience is unlikely to see Romeo and Juliet until they are, as if by magic, alone together. Romeo has placed himself so that he would naturally have the next dance with Juliet. As the others are engaged in this, he leads Juliet apart (see lines 48-9, 130). Before he speaks, the dancers have moved backstage; he has taken off his visor.

The rhyme, meter, and interwoven imagery of the sonnet Romeo and Juliet speak together sets the tone of their meeting; it encourages a quiet, careful tenderness and a sense of awe (especially supported by the religious images). After line 98, the lovers place their palms together, which involves a formal pose of confrontation and acceptance to match the formality of their speeches. At the same time, their faces have been brought close together, so that intimacy is increased. At this point, they mostly have only one line each at a time, and phrases are shorter: so, without speaking more quickly, the pace seems faster and stronger, as if both their hearts beat together in anticipation and excitement. Meanwhile, the keener wordplay gives an impression of quickened sensibility and shared delight.

After line 104, the lovers are silent as they kiss. In the center of the crowded stage, amid dancing, attendance, and threatened violence, Shakespeare has so directed the audience's attention that the heart of the drama can be this silent kiss, a token of giving and receiving in love and trust. When John Neville and Claire Bloom played the lovers at the Old Vic, London, "They drew irresistibly closer, their hands touched, their eyes held each other, and the very stillness of the air seemed to sing with love" (*Daily Mail*, 13 June, 1956).

**105-18** Romeo and Juliet stay together to speak a further quatrain and kiss again. The wit has quickened and, this time, Juliet may initiate the kiss.

Probably the dancing ends just before the nurse comes to Juliet. Romeo puts on his visor again and Juliet runs off. There is a great deal of movement and business on-stage and probably unspecified talk and laughter among the guests as Romeo questions the nurse; this all contrasts with his stunned recognition that his new love is also his "foe". He does not answer the nurse; she probably hurries off before he speaks the tense, savage soliloquy of lines 115-6. As he stands alone and helpless, Benvolio hurries up to him. To him, Romeo speaks with a bitter sense of what must now happen; he feels powerless or is unwilling to resist his fate.

**119-25** Capulet comes forward busily, but he is

Is it e'en so?° Why then, I thank you all.
I thank you, honest° gentlemen. Good night.
More torches here! Come on, then let's to bed.
Ah sirrah, by my fay,° it waxes° late;
I'll to my rest. [*Exeunt all but* Juliet *and* Nurse.]

Juliet Come hither, Nurse. What is yond gentleman?

Nurse The son and heir of old Tiberio.

Juliet What's he that now is going out of door?

Nurse Marry, that I think be young Petrucio.

Juliet What's he that follows there, that would not dance?

Nurse I know not.

Juliet Go ask his name.—If he be marrièd,
My grave is like to be my wedding bed.

Nurse His name is Romeo, and a Montague;
The only son of your great enemy.

Juliet My only love, sprung from my only hate!
Too early seen unknown, and known too late!
Prodigious° birth of love it is to me
That I must love a loathèd enemy.

Nurse What's this, what's this?

Juliet A rhyme I learnt even now
Of one I danced withal. *One calls within,* "Juliet."

Nurse Anon,° anon!
Come let's away. The strangers all are gone. *Exeunt.*

(the maskers insist on leaving)
worthy

faith grows

now tired. Taking time to collect cloaks, torches, visors, and bid farewell to their dance partners, the maskers depart, Romeo once again one amongst them. Meanwhile Juliet comes forward on-stage and then calls for the nurse.

**126-42** Juliet, hiding her feelings instinctively, at first pretends she is interested in other guests and maskers. In many productions, she moves away from the nurse before speaking lines 136-9 as a wondering, despairing soliloquy of spontaneous strength. At this moment, she, like Romeo in I.iv, foresees a bitter consequence of her new love, but she also affirms its power and life. After line 136, Julia Marlowe as Juliet "sat and looked far into space on the gathering fates" (C. E. Russell, *Julia Marlowe*, 1926, p. 231).

As the nurse hurries up to her, Juliet almost hides her feeling again; only now the excuse she invents expresses something of her joy and wonder as she transposes the meeting with Romeo into a dance and her foreboding into a mere "rhyme". It is at this point that a voice from offstage summons her, and she has to face her future.

ominous/amazing/unnatural

So the focus is on Juliet for the last moments of the first Act. The stage is nearly empty after the festivities and, in the new quietness, the audience will attend carefully. If Juliet stays unmoving and thoughtful as the nurse moves towards the door, speaking as if to a child, the last sentence of the scene can sound pathetically ironic. As Juliet looks at the place where she met Romeo or where she last saw him in a doorway, or as she looks to see where she must go, she says nothing: hesitation, her movement across the wide stage, and her physical bearing can express gentle, impulsive, and strong feelings, in a way that invites the audience's own imaginative understanding.

at once

At the end of the scene, Miss O'Neill as Juliet, was so "rivetted to the ground" that even when the nurse "drags her away...her eye is seen to look to the door" through which Romeo had gone (C. I. Jones, *Memoirs*, 1816, pp. 13-4).

# ACT II

*Enter* Chorus.

Chorus Now old desire° doth in his deathbed lie,
And young affection° gapes° to be his heir;
That fair for which love° groaned for and would die,
With tender Juliet matched,° is now not fair.
Now Romeo is beloved, and loves again,
Alike bewitchèd by the charm° of looks;
But to his foe supposed° he must complain,°
And she steal love's sweet bait from fearful hooks.°
Being held a foe, he may not have access
To breathe such vows as lovers use° to swear,
And she as much in love, her means much less
To meet her new belovèd any where.
But passion lends them power, time means to meet,
Temp'ring extremities° with extreme sweet. [*Exit*.]

## Scene i *Enter* Romeo *alone*.

Romeo Can I go forward when my heart is here?
Turn back, dull earth,° and find thy center° out.
[Romeo *retires*.]

*Enter* Benvolio *with* Mercutio.

Benvolio Romeo! My cousin Romeo! Romeo!

Mercutio He is wise
And, on my life, hath stol'n him home to bed.

Benvolio He ran this way and leapt this orchard wall.

## ACT II

i.e., for Rosaline

new love (for Juliet) longs

the lover

compared

enchantment

presumed lament

(like a fish, she tries to take the tasty bait off the hook without being caught)

are accustomed

alleviating extreme adversities

**1-14** If the Chorus enters and takes command of the stage with a slow dignity in keeping with the stiff and stately sonnet that he speaks, the effect will be to hold back the audience's expectation and encourage them to reflect on the dramatic events.

This omniscient spokesman can keep in mind his own earlier prediction of a star-crossed fate (Prol., 6) so that, when he now speaks of the death of "old desire" and the greediness of "love," the audience may foresee the greater and final catastrophe as if for themselves. Such response is sustained by "bewitched…foe…bait…fearful," and then the two clashing "extremities" of the last line.

The Elizabethan theater had neither stage curtain nor the device of blackout and so, while the Chorus speaks, attendants probably clear away the stools and other paraphernalia used in the previous ball scene.

### Scene i

insensitive body (opposed to *heart*) i.e., *dull*, or heavy, earth is attracted by force of gravity to its *center*, or *heart*

**1-6** Romeo runs on stage and then off again in the same direction. In modern productions, he will often enter through a door and then return by leaping over an "orchard wall" (see l. 5). In Elizabethan performances, he might have climbed part of the stage structure. Immediately after this, Benvolio and Mercutio enter and, usually, they are accompanied by other maskers. Everything takes place as if in darkness and so torches may be carried.

When Romeo appears alone at the start of this new Act and after the Chorus's introduction, the audience may well expect a soliloquy, but he is too distraught or amazed: he speaks only two verse-lines

Call, good Mercutio.

MERCUTIO Nay, I'll conjure° too.
Romeo! Humors!° Madman! Passion! Lover!
Appear thou in the likeness of a sigh;
Speak but one rhyme, and I am satisfied;
Cry but "Ay me!", pronounce but "love" and "dove";
Speak to my gossip° Venus one fair word,
One nickname for her purblind° son and heir,
Young Abraham° Cupid, he that shot so true
When King Cophetua loved the beggar maid!—
He heareth not, he stirreth not, he moveth not:
The ape is dead,° and I must conjure him.—
I conjure thee by Rosaline's bright eyes,
By her high forehead, and her scarlet lip,
By her fine foot, straight leg, and quivering thigh,
And the demesnes° that there adjacent lie,
That in thy likeness thou appear to us!

BENVOLIO And if he hear thee, thou wilt anger him.

MERCUTIO This cannot anger him: 'twould anger him
To raise° a spirit in his mistress' circle°
Of some strange nature, letting it there stand
Till she had laid it° and conjured it down;
That were some spite. My invocation
Is fair and honest:° and in his mistress' name,
I conjure only but to raise up him.

BENVOLIO Come, he hath hid himself among these trees
To be consorted° with the humorous° night:
Blind is his love, and best befits the dark.

MERCUTIO If love be blind, love cannot hit the mark.°
Now will he sit under a medlar tree,
And wish his mistress were that kind of fruit
As maids call medlars° when they laugh alone.
O Romeo, that she were, O that she were
An open-arse° and thou a pop'rin pear!°
Romeo good night. I'll to my truckle° bed;
This field° bed is too cold for me to sleep.
Come, shall we go?

BENVOLIO Go then, for 'tis in vain
To seek him here that means not to be found.

*Exit* [*with* Mercutio.]

call up spirits by magic incantation

moods, affections

(and those without a rhyme). His words seem to be stopped by unspoken thoughts: desire, fear, determination, "extreme sweet" (II, Prol., 14) all jangle together.

good friend (flippant)

totally blind

cheat/blind patriarch

i.e., Romeo plays dead, like a performing ape

private territories

**7-21** Although Benvolio had entered leading the search, now Mercutio springs to life pretending to conjure for Romeo. As in the Queen Mab speech, the actor can mimic the various creatures of Mercutio's fantasy. He probably starts by adopting the exaggerated gestures and strange voice of a cheating conjurer and proceeds to be mad, impassioned, fighing, and, finally, a confident Cupid; he then deflates all that pretense with the factual line 15. Mercutio does not take silence for an answer. Pretending to conjure to raise Romeo from death (see I. 16), he becomes still more weirdly commanding and this leads him on to describe Rosalind in terms calculated to arouse Romeo sexually, should he be hiding and listening, and cause him to protest at the liberties his friend is taking.

Other maskers usually applaud and augment Mercutio's efforts. When the play was performed in daylight in the Elizabethan public theater, reactions to the supposed darkness would have heightened both the horseplay and an underlying unease in the outrageous mockery.

i.e., sexually excite

magical circle (sexual innuendo)

appeased it by magic/sexually satisfied it

chaste

keep company

humid/moody

target

(pun on *meddle* = have sex)

(country name for medlar fruit)

(variety of pear: bawdy)

on castors

camp/in the open air

**22-42** Mercutio responds to Benvolio's caution with more mockery which further develops the sexual awareness and the pretense of superiority. By line 30, Benvolio has decided to give up the search; this only heightens Mercutio's counterreaction.

Some Mercutios address lines 39-40 to the absent Romeo, assuming that a he is listening: they imply he is a fool to stay out in the "cold." Then Benvolio's final words can be said as a reprooof to the absent Romeo.

As they all go off, they may laugh, catcall, or yawn broadly. Some pauses, a single moment of watchful stillness (they are looking for Romeo), or an overplaying of the jokes, together a response to the darkness, can give to this scene the air of a party running down. The scene had started vociferously in seeking Romeo but finishes with self-consolation and a decision to leave him to his own devices; they have not been rewarded by any response to their efforts.

Scene ii [Romeo *comes forward*.]

Romeo He° jests at scars that never felt a wound.

[*Enter* Juliet *at a window*.]

But, soft,° what light through yonder window breaks?
It is the East, and Juliet is the sun!
Arise, fair sun, and kill the envious moon,
Who is already sick and pale with grief
That thou her maid° art far more fair than she.
Be not her maid, since she is envious:
Her vestal° livery is but sick and green,°
And none but fools do wear it: cast it off.
It is my lady! O it is my love!
O that she knew she were!
She speaks, yet she says nothing. What of that?
Her eye discourses;° I will answer it.
I am too bold; 'tis not to me she speaks.
Two of the fairest stars in all the heaven,
Having some business, do entreat her eyes
To twinkle in their spheres° till they return.
What if her eyes were there, they in her head?
The brightness of her cheek would shame those stars,
As daylight doth a lamp; her eyes in heaven
Would through the airy region° stream so bright
That birds would sing, and think it were not night.
See how she leans her cheek upon her hand:
O that I were a glove upon that hand,
That I might touch that cheek!

Juliet Ay me!

Romeo She speaks.
O speak again, bright angel, for thou art
As glorious to this night, being o'er my head,
As is a wingèd messenger of heaven
Unto the white-upturnèd° wond'ring eyes

## Scene ii

i.e., a man like Mercutio

be quiet

(virgins were the maids of Diana, the moon goddess)

virginal anemic (play on the motley green dress of court fools)

speaks

orbits

(of the sky)

looking up, so that the whites only are seen on earth

**1** The rhyme of Romeo's first line with the last line of the previous scene suggests that he enters as Benvolio runs off. But the location has changed: Romeo is now on the other side of the orchard wall. He walks as if on enemy territory at night and is aware at once of any movement or light. It was said of Garrick's Romeo that he came "creeping in upon his toes, whispering his love and looking about him just like a thief in the night" (W. Cooke, *Memoirs of Macklin*, 1804, p. 205).

The "Balcony Scene" which now follows is a uniquely sustained duologue: danger, tenderness, ecstasy, longing, and delight are all sensitively presented in a setting of quiet night. The lovers are separated from each other by the raised window or balcony of Juliet's bedroom, and this adds to the urgency of their talk which must be kept quiet to prevent anyone overhearing.

A freshness and intimacy in the duologue enable performers like John Gielgud and Peggy Ashcroft to act as if it were all happening for the very first time: "Romeo seems to stand apart, wrapped in himself, in wondering contemplation of the tryst, of Juliet's attitudes, of the melody of their voices and the loveliness of the moonlight...There is impatience in his speech. He likes the long silences. Juliet, on the other hand, is self-forgotten, seeing nothing, hearing nothing, except Romeo..." (M. Sayers, *New English Weekly*, 12 Dec., 1935).

Silence and slowness can be particularly effective in this intimate scene. Sometimes it is Juliet who holds back her words: so, in a performance of 1896, as soon as Romeo has said, "He jests at scars that never felt a wound" (l. 1), Julia Marlowe as Juliet "came slowly out upon the balcony, looking in the moonlight more like a beautiful apparition than a creature of mortality. She sighed gently and seated herself on a stool, leaning on the balcony." Her first soliloquy was "soft and meditative" (C. E. Russell, *Julia Marlowe*, 1926, p. 232).

**2-11** Romeo speaks quietly, but his excitement is betrayed in short, strongly phrased exclamations (ll. 4, 10). Recognizing Juliet, he delights in her beauty and sun-like power; then, in the next moment, remembers her virginity. The short line 11 suggests a pause during which Romeo gazes, saying nothing.

**12-25** At line 13, Romeo is about to go to the window, but then stops. As he does so, his imagination gathers strength with lengthening rhythms and air-

Of mortals that fall back to gaze on him,
When he bestrides the lazy-pacing clouds
And sails upon the bosom of the air.

JULIET O Romeo, Romeo, wherefore art thou Romeo?
Deny° thy father and refuse° thy name;
Or, if thou wilt not, be but sworn my love,
And I'll no longer be a Capulet.

ROMEO [*Aside.*] Shall I hear more, or shall I speak at this?

JULIET 'Tis but thy name that is my enemy.
Thou art thyself, though not° a Montague.
What's Montague? It is nor hand, nor foot,
Nor arm, nor face, nor any other part
Belonging to a man. O be some other name.
What's in a name? That which we call a rose
By any other word would smell as sweet.
So Romeo would, were he not Romeo called,
Retain that dear perfection which he owes°
Without that title. Romeo doff° thy name;
And for° thy name, which is no part of thee,
Take all myself.

ROMEO I take thee at thy word.°
Call me but love, and I'll be new baptized;
Henceforth I never will be Romeo.

JULIET What man art thou, that thus bescreened in night,
So stumblest on my counsel?°

ROMEO By a name
I know not how to tell thee who I am.
My name, dear saint, is hateful to myself
Because it is an enemy to thee.
Had I it written, I would tear the word.

JULIET My ears have not yet drunk a hundred words
Of that tongue's uttering, yet I know the sound.
Art thou not Romeo, and a Montague?

ROMEO Neither, fair maid, if either thee dislike.°

JULIET How camest thou hither, tell me, and wherefore?°
The orchard walls are high and hard to climb,

borne, celestial fantasies. Only when he looks more closely—perhaps, after a moment's fear on "night" of line 22—and as he remembers where he is, does he begin to think again of himself (l. 24).

disown     renounce

**25-32** Juliet's sigh (l. 25) brings immediate recognition and response, but she cannot see or hear him. Romeo, eager to hear more, now speaks of Juliet as "bright angel" in the most sustained image thus far in the scene. Spoken quietly, these words can seem to hang in the air; the image is both fanciful and real, as Romeo looks up with "wondering eyes."

even if you were not

**33-9** The audience's attention has been caught and held by occasional silences, the description of line 23, the sigh, and Romeo's attentiveness. So Juliet can now speak slowly and deliberately; her words are direct and simple, but she repeats Romeo's name with a new wonder and loving gentleness. Line 33 is so effective in its context that it has become one of the most famous in the play. Romeo's aside (l. 37) can be spoken after Juliet has relapsed into silent thought.

owns

put off

in exchange for

However, the more impulsive Juliets of the nineteen-nineties have found a more forceful way of acting this moment, expressing their frustration with family restrictions and impatience with Romeo.

at once/as you offer yourself

**40-53** As Juliet answers her own question, the phrasing suggests a quicker pace and a quickening imagination. First at line 42, and then at line 47, she addresses an imaginary Romeo, the second time concluding with the total and simple committal of "Take all myself." On hearing this, in a moment, Romeo makes contact and Juliet's imaginary world collapses, so that her next lines are in complete contrast: careful, apprehensive, and insecure. She seems wholly unprepared for what Romeo is actually saying or, even, to hear his name (l. 51).

private thoughts

**53-60** Romeo eagerly answers yet hesitates to use his name. Probably "dear saint" is a conscious quotation from the words they exchanged when they had first met (see I.v. 91-104). This reassures Juliet and she speaks with renewed quickening of imagination, shown in the use of the physical word "drunk:" her love is palpable, felt as the act of drinking is felt. She now gives him back his name, even though conscious that it belongs to her family's enemy.

displease

why

**61-78** In a moment, recognition is complete; they stand silently, each held in the other's gaze. Then Juliet starts, and will continue, to ask practical ques-

And the place death, considering who thou art,
If any of my kinsmen find thee here.

ROMEO With love's light wings did I o'erperch° these walls,
For stony limits cannot hold love out,
And what love can do, that dares love attempt:
Therefore thy kinsmen are no stop to me.

JULIET If they do see thee, they will murder thee.

ROMEO Alack there lies more peril in thine eye
Than twenty of their swords; look thou but sweet,
And I am proof° against their enmity.

JULIET I would not for the world they saw thee here.

ROMEO I have night's cloak to hide me from their eyes.
And but° thou love me, let them find me here:
My life were better ended by their hate
Than death proroguèd,° wanting of thy love.

JULIET By whose direction found'st thou out this place?

ROMEO By Love, that first did prompt me to inquire:
He lent me counsel, and I lent him eyes°.
I am no pilot, yet, wert thou as far
As that vast shore washed with the farthest sea,°
I should adventure° for such merchandise.

JULIET Thou knowest the mask of night is on my face,
Else would a maiden blush bepaint my cheek
For that which thou hast heard me speak tonight.
Fain° would I dwell on form;° fain, fain deny
What I have spoke. But farewell compliment!°
Doest thou love me? I know thou wilt say "Ay";
And I will take° thy word. Yet if thou swear'st,
Thou mayst prove false. At lovers' perjuries,
They say Jove laughs. O gentle Romeo,
If thou dost love, pronounce° it faithfully.
Or if thou thinkest I am too quickly won,
I'll frown and be perverse, and say thee nay,
So° thou wilt woo; but else, not for the world.
In truth, fair Montague, I am too fond,°
And therefore thou mayst think my havior° light;°

surmount*

tions and to urge caution. Romeo answers fantastically but always with a daring and urgent affirmation of his love. Much depends on how the actor speaks the lines: Romeo can appear elated, careless of everything except his happiness in Juliet's presence; or he can be determined to assert his will; or he can play recklessly with danger and so sharpen his response to the moment. When he imagines his own death (ll. 77-8), he can seem either desperate, or instinctively doomed, or simply and, even, happily reckless; he is caught up in his imagination with thoughts of Juliet and of his love for her.

invulnerable to

if only

deferred

(because Love is blindfolded)

(alluding to the journey toward Death's kingdom)

risk all/journey

**79-84** Juliet's response is very practical but he answers with a "vast" image for his love that is sustained throughout lines 82-84 and provides a climactic assertion of his devotion against the certainty of death: its effect can be that of a solemn pledge.

Juliet accepts his avowal silently and she may pause before replying in a quite different mood.

gladly keep within limits of conventional behavior

etiquette

accept

declare

**85-106** Juliet thinks, and probably speaks, rapidly now. She almost apologizes for herself, her modesty, hesitation, eagerness. Then, in an unguarded moment, she asks if he loves her and, quite as quickly, prevents his reply. She quotes common talk (ll. 92-3) and, to disprove it, asks him to declare his faithfulness. Yet she cannot leave it there, but instinctively imagines misunderstandings and again pledges her truth. Perhaps she does not pause at all during this speech; if she were to do so, Romeo will seem bemused in his silence, through joy or through lack of adequate reply; perhaps he tries to respond and is unable to do so.

if only

affectionate/foolish behavior light-headed/immodest

But trust me, gentleman, I'll prove more true
Than those that have more cunning to be strange.°
I should have been more strange, I must confess,
But that thou overheard'st, ere I was ware,°
My truelove passion.° Therefore pardon me,
And not impute this yielding to light° love,
Which the dark° night hath so discoverèd°.

ROMEO Lady, by yonder blessèd moon I vow,
That tips with silver all these fruit-tree tops—

JULIET O swear not by the moon, th' inconstant moon,
That monthly changes in her circled orb,
Lest that thy love prove likewise variable.

ROMEO What shall I swear by?

JULIET Do not swear at all.
Or if thou wilt, swear by thy gracious self
Which is the god of my idolatry,
And I'll believe thee.

ROMEO If my heart's dear love—

JULIET Well, do not swear. Although I joy in thee,
I have no joy of this contract° tonight;
It is too rash, too unadvised,° too sudden,
Too like the lightning which doth cease to be
Ere one can say it lightens. Sweet, good night!
This bud of love, by summer's ripening breath,
May prove a beauteous flow'r when next we meet.
Good night, good night! As sweet repose and rest
Come to thy heart, as that° within my breast!

ROMEO O wilt thou leave me so unsatisfied?

JULIET What satisfaction canst thou have tonight?

ROMEO Th' exchange of thy love's faithful vow for mine.

JULIET I gave thee mine before thou didst request it.
And yet I would it were to give again.

ROMEO Wouldst thou withdraw it? For what purpose, love?

JULIET But to be frank° and give it thee again.

distant, reserved

aware

outburst

wanton

(wordplay on *light,* line 105)
revealed

**107-24** At last, Romeo is able to reply. He starts formally, with "Lady" instead of "fair maid" or "dear saint," and with a description that suggests he has become aware of the whole context of their meeting, finding it rich, tender, and elevated beyond any common experience.

When Juliet cuts him short at line 109, the momentary effect can be comic. She may speak now because she is afraid; and, certainly, by line 116 this has become explicit in her words. After the image of destructive lightning, she suddenly bids "good night," and he stands speechless. She must see his concern, because her next words are tender and more reassuring. Then, as if her fears have returned, she is more insistent with repeated "good night"s. Once more tenderness returns, only now she looks forward no further than the present night.

exchange of vows

unconsidered

**125-48** When Romeo speaks again, it is to complain and ask for clarification, but his meaning is ambiguous, as Juliet immediately recognizes. Perhaps he did mean to ask for a mutual betrothal as he says at l. 127, but not all Romeos and Juliets make this assumption.

as to that heart which is

Once the uncertainty has been resolved, both lovers talk with new urgency, which, in turn at line 130, leads Romeo to be unsure of her meaning. It is this doubt that provokes Juliet's "frank" reassurance and awakens her most resonant avowal of love and endless happiness (ll. 133-5). Here she uses images and concepts that are often found in Shakespeare's sonnets and comedies where they express the overflowing richness of self-giving love; here, however, reference to the sea may betray an intimation of death.

free, generous

At line 135, a mutual silence is established, so that the nurse is audible backstage. Juliet, no longer eager to escape (as at lines 120 and 123), goes off

And yet I wish but for the thing I have:
My bounty is as boundless as the sea,
My love as deep; the more I give to thee,
The more I have, for both are infinite.
I hear some noise within. Dear love, adieu!
[NURSE *calls within.*]
Anon,° good Nurse! Sweet Montague, be true.
Stay but a little, I will come again. [*Exit.*]

ROMEO O blessèd, blessèd night! I am afeard,
Being in night, all this is but a dream,
Too flattering-sweet to be substantial.°

[*Enter* JULIET *again.*]

JULIET Three words, dear ROMEO, and good night indeed.
If that thy bent° of love be honorable,
Thy purpose marriage, send me word tomorrow,
By one that I'll procure° to come to thee,
Where and what time thou wilt perform the rite;
And all my fortunes° at thy foot I'll lay
And follow thee, my lord, throughout the world.
[NURSE (*Within*).] Madam!

JULIET I come, anon.°—But if thou meanest not well,
I do beseech thee— [NURSE (*Within*).] Madam!
By and by,° I come.—
To cease thy strife,° and leave me to my grief.
Tomorrow will I send.

ROMEO So thrive my soul°—

JULIET A thousand times good night! [*Exit.*]

ROMEO A thousand times the worse, to want° thy light!
Love goes toward love as schoolboys from their books;
But love from love, toward school with heavy looks.

*Enter* JULIET *again.*

JULIET Hist, Romeo, hist! O, for a falc'ner's voice
To lure° this tassel gentle° back again!

promising to return. The rhyme on "adieu" and "true" shows that she has remembered earlier fears and assertions (see ll. 90-1, 94, 100, 104, etc.). She probably intends to leave as she speaks the rhyme, but then her eagerness and willingness to take risks are reasserted in the unrhymed line which she adds as if it were an afterthought.

coming

**139-48** Romeo's short soliloquy (ll. 139-41) can be spoken as if he is dazed; his conscious understanding is trying to catch up with his awakened fantasy and pleasure. Probably he stays quite still, as if "afeard" of breaking the spell. In contrast, Juliet on her return is practical and precise, as well as tender. "My lord" suggests that she here takes a small, formal step toward marriage.

real

In Zeffirelli's Old Vic production of 1960, "there was a still silence" on Juliet's return to the stage after the nurse had called her away; it was some time before she dared to speak or Romeo come out of hiding (line 142). This mutual sense of awe and fear in the realization of their newfound love was given meaning by Romeo's preceding lines (139-41) and prepared for the urgent request for confirmation in Juliet's next words (*Shakespeare Survey*, 1962, p. 148).

aim, force (as of a *bent* bow)

arrange

possessions / fortune

at once

**149-56** As the nurse calls more loudly and frequently, Juliet tries to answer her calmly and interject brief instructions to Romeo in urgent whispers. With a renewed sense of danger, her fear that Romeo may be false (l. 149) returns; it is dispelled as soon as he begins to speak (l. 152). His vow, only four words, is expressed so fervently that it satisfies Juliet.

immediately

striving

as I hope to be saved

Again left alone, Romeo is now assured enough to reflect on his state of mind, using proverbs as if trying to make his experience seem less extraordinary and more manageable. Very slowly he starts to leave.

lack

recall (a term of falconry)
male peregrine falcon

**157-65** In some productions, Romeo has almost left the stage before Juliet reappears; in others, he

Bondage is hoarse,° and may not speak aloud,
Else would I tear the cave° where Echo° lies
And make her airy tongue more hoarse than mine
With repetition of my "Romeo!"

ROMEO It is my soul that calls upon my name.
How silver-sweet sound lovers' tongues by night,
Like softest music to attending° ears.

JULIET Romeo!

ROMEO My sweet?

JULIET What o'clock tomorrow
Shall I send to thee?

ROMEO By the hour of nine.

JULIET I will not fail; 'tis twenty year till then.
I have forgot why I did call thee back.

ROMEO Let me stand here till thou remember it.

JULIET I shall forget, to have thee still° stand there,
Rememb'ring how I love thy company.

ROMEO And I'll still stay, to have thee still forget,
Forgetting any other home but this.

JULIET 'Tis almost morning. I would have thee gone—
And yet no further than a wanton's° bird,
That lets it hop a little from his hand,
Like a poor prisoner in his twisted gyves,°
And with a silken thread° plucks it back again,
So loving-jealous of his liberty.

ROMEO I would I were thy bird.

JULIET Sweet, so would I;
Yet I should kill thee with much cherishing.
Good night, good night! Parting is such sweet sorrow,
That I shall say good night till it be morrow.° [*Exit.*]

ROMEO Sleep dwell upon thine eyes, peace in thy breast!
Would I were sleep and peace, so sweet to rest!
Hence will I to my ghostly° friar's close° cell,

I am watched and must whisper

pierce the air (a nymph who, according to Ovid, pined for Narcissus until only her voice was left)

has stayed rooted to the spot and for that reason Juliet cannot see him.

As Juliet strains to see or hear Romeo, her imagery is of the chase and imprisonment. He is so lost in his delight at her return that he probably continues to speak in soliloquy; his images are spiritual and delicate. As John Gielgud played the character, the words flowed "in an even stream, one thought merging delicately into the next"; Laurence Olivier, taking over the part in the same production, spoke with more point, "It is my soul that calls upon my name..." and "by planting attention on a problematical soul, lessened the value of the lines following" (*Tatler*, 11 Dec., 1935).

attentive*

**166-74** The lovers' recognition is quick and simple. By lines 169-72, both can be silent; yet they gently play with each other's words as if fondling each other in thought.

always

**174-84** Romeo's "home" reminds Juliet of danger, and the spell is abruptly broken as she, gently now, urges him to go—and yet stay her prisoner. Line 182 may be another intimation of death. Some Juliets weep silently, through joy and sadness; most break away and run off on the rhyme.

playful child's

shackles

(tied to its leg)

morning

spiritual secluded, private

**187-88** Romeo is now alert; he has broken from his dream-like mood with a quick recognition of his

His help to crave, and my dear hap° to tell. *Exit.*

Scene iii *Enter* Friar Lawrence *alone, with a basket.*

Friar The gray-eyed morn smiles on the frowning night,
Check'ring the eastern clouds with streaks of light;
And fleckèd° darkness like a drunkard reels
From forth day's path and Titan's° burning wheels.
Now ere the sun advance his burning eye,
The day to cheer and night's dank dew to dry,
I must upfill this osier cage° of ours
With baleful weeds and precious-juicèd flowers.
The earth that's nature's mother is her tomb;
What is her burying grave, that is her womb:°
And from her womb children° of divers kind
We sucking on her natural bosom find,
Many for many virtues excellent,
None but for some,° and yet all different.
O mickle° is the powerful grace° that lies
In plants, herbs, stones, and their true qualities;
For naught so vile that on the earth doth live
But to the earth some special good doth give;
Nor aught so good but, strained° from that fair use,
Revolts from true birth,° stumbling on abuse.°
Virtue itself turns° vice, being misapplied,
And vice sometime's by action dignified.°

*Enter* Romeo.

Within the infant° rind of this weak flower
Poison hath residence, and medicine power:
For this, being smelt, with that part° cheers each part;°
Being tasted, slays all senses with the heart.°
Two such opposèd kings encamp them still°
In man as well as herbs—grace and rude will;°
And where the worser is predominant,
Full soon the canker° death eats up that plant.

good fortune

longing for Juliet that he expresses in plans for immediate action. In contrast to his earlier exit at lines 155-6, he now leaves quickly.

Scene iii

**1-22** The friar enters alone, like the Chorus had done, and so gains close attention, but he is careful, not commanding. This soliloquy is in contrast with the preceding scene: night, no longer blessed, is a reeling "drunkard"; it is now early dawn, and at first there is no immediate, pressing action or conflict; rhyming couplets and frequent antitheses carry the words forward smoothly without pause.

The audience seems to be addressed directly, somewhat in the manner of a meditation or sermon. The friar's subjects are the transitoriness of life, the presence of good in every creature no matter how "vile", and the risk of virtue turning to evil. The whole speech may be intended by Shakespeare as a means of encouraging the audience's sober reflection on the story of the play thus far. However, in some productions, the friar is fussy and rather smug, as if he knows nothing except how to deal with weeds and flowers; the effect of this interpretation is to isolate the lovers more completely from their elders.

flushed, reddened

Hyperion's (he drove his chariot, the sun, across the sky)

willow basket

natural growths come from the earth and, when dead, are absorbed by it again

i.e., plants

all nature's products have some virtues

great (archaic) divine power

forced

its proper nature misuse

turns into

made worthy

**23-31** As the friar picks up a small flower and so draws the audience's close attention, Romeo enters silently: he probably stands recovering his breath, having run all the way to the cell. He speaks as soon as the friar draws to a close with thoughts of "death," but he may not have heard what has been said, and certainly makes no reference to it. Nevertheless, the audience may hear the friar's words as a criticism of Romeo that challenges its earlier judgement of him.

tender

quality the whole man

stops the heart and all senses with it

always

fleshly desires

maggot

ROMEO Good morrow, father.

FRIAR *Benedicite?*°
What early tongue so sweet saluteth me?
Young son, it argues a distemperèd° head
So soon to bid good morrow to thy bed.
Care keeps his watch° in every old man's eye,
And where care lodges, sleep will never lie;
But where unbruisèd° youth with unstuffed brain
Doth couch his limbs, there golden sleep doth reign.
Therefore thy earliness doth me assure
Thou art uproused with some distemp'rature.°
Or if not so—then here I hit it right—
Our Romeo hath not been in bed tonight.

ROMEO That last is true: the sweeter rest was mine.

FRIAR God pardon sin! Wast thou with Rosaline?

ROMEO With Rosaline, my ghostly° father? No.
I have forgot that name, and that name's woe.

FRIAR That's my good son! But where hast thou been then?

ROMEO I'll tell thee ere thou ask it me again.
I have been feasting with mine enemy,
Where on a sudden one hath wounded me,
That's by me wounded. Both our remedies
Within thy help and holy physic° lies.
I bear no hatred, blessèd man: for lo,
My intercession likewise steads° my foe.

FRIAR Be plain, good son, and homely° in thy drift:
Riddling confession finds but riddling shrift.°

ROMEO Then plainly know, my heart's dear love is set
On the fair daughter of rich Capulet;
As mine on hers, so hers is set on mine,
And all combined,° save what thou must combine°
By holy marriage. When and where, and how,
We met, we wooed, and made exchange of vow,
I'll tell thee as we pass;° but this I pray,
That thou consent to marry us today.

FRIAR Holy Saint Francis, what a change is here!

bless you

troubled

vigil

unhurt, inexperienced

disturbance of the mind

spiritual

i.e., sacramental power of marriage

helps

straightforward

absolution

agreed join together

go along

**31-42** The friar is so engrossed in his own thoughts that, although he immediately blesses his visitor (he usually makes the sign of the cross), he does not recognize him at first. This self-absorption prepares the audience for the friar's fatal inability to respond to Juliet's needs when the watch break into the tomb (V.iii.158-9). Some friars, however, only pretend not to recognize Romeo and so imply criticism of his impulsiveness (see l. 94); played in this way, the friar may have noted Romeo's entry and intended lines 23-30 as a direct warning to his "son."

As the friar continues to expound on the habits of youth, using rhyme and antitheses to score his points, Romeo will grow impatient and may attempt to interrupt after lines 34 and 40.

**43** Romeo's response ignores all the friar's moralistic criticism to express his own contentment.

**44-47** Romeo's "No" is usually spoken with sudden and astonished emphasis, before begininng to explain that all is changed for him. Some Romeos complete the couplet in the same assertive way; others as if patiently explaining something that should have been self-evident; others are completely caught up, once more, in a deep sense of pleasure and achievement. Played in any of these ways, the contrast between Romeo's couplet and the friar's questioning response will cause the audience to laugh at Romeo or the friar, or at both of them.

**48-64** Romeo can now say what he has come to say and, perhaps, imply a rebuke to the friar for jumping to conclusions. As Romeo expresses delight and wonder to the friar's bewilderment, there is more opportunity for comedy in the contrast between youth and careful age. When he speaks "plainly," his rhythms quicken and he hurries to say what he wants (l. 64); this is expressed with an absolute simplicity that can be intense or comically blunt and unreflective.

At several points the friar may wish to interject, but Romeo leaves no opportunity for this until he has got to the heart of his message and its call for an immediate response.

**65-80** It is Romeo's turn to stand speechless as the friar admonishes with heavy sarcasm. The actor

Is Rosaline, whom thou didst love so dear,
So soon forsaken? Young men's love then lies
Not truly in their hearts, but in their eyes.°
Jesu Maria, what a deal of brine°
Hath washed thy sallow cheeks for Rosaline!
How much salt water thrown away in waste
To season° love, that of it doth not taste!
The sun not yet thy sighs° from heaven clears,
Thy old groans ring yet in my ancient ears.
Lo here upon thy cheek the stain doth sit
Of an old tear that is not washed off yet.
If e'er thou wast thyself, and these woes thine,
Thou and these woes were all for Rosaline.
And art thou changed? Pronounce this sentence° then:
Women may fall° when there's no strength in men.

ROMEO Thou chid'st me oft for loving Rosaline.

FRIAR For doting, not for loving, pupil mine.

ROMEO And bad'st me bury love.

FRIAR Not in a grave
To lay one in, another out to have.

ROMEO I pray thee chide me not. Her I love now
Doth grace° for grace, and love for love allow.
The other did not so.

FRIAR O she knew well
Thy love did read by rote, and could not spell.°
But come young waverer, come go with me.
In one respect° I'll thy assistant be;
For this alliance may so happy prove
To turn your households' rancor to pure love.

ROMEO O let us hence! I stand° on sudden haste.

FRIAR Wisely and slow. They stumble that run fast. *Exeunt.*

must choose how to respond: most Romeos are comically helpless or impatiently inattentive; a quiet, still response, however, can make the friar appear foolishly overconfident.

is superficial, based on appearance

salt tears

Line 75 implies that the two are now sitting (or standing) very close together, implying some measure of submission in Romeo.

preserve / flavor

(imagined as clouds)

maxim

be fickle

**81-94** In this rapid interchange, the friar teases Romeo (ll. 84, 88); sometimes he is gentle and even sympathetic, but other friars still further sharpen their criticism. Lines 91-2 introduce a new note: the friar has been considering carefully what he should do and speaks now without irony or reproof.

Romeo maintains a serious simplicity until his last line, when he is so eager to go into the friar's cell that he does not stop to thank him. This delighted, spontaneous, and physical response, offset by the friar's last lines, is the climax to the scene. Yet, for all his excitement, Romeo must wait for the friar to lead the way (and sometimes he takes time to gather up his basket and herbs), and so, despite the potential comedy of the situation, the friar's last words can be effective as a hint of disaster to come.

favor

you babbled of love, not knowing the language

on account of one thing

depend

Scene iv *Enter* Benvolio *and* Mercutio.

Mercutio Where the devil should° this Romeo be?
Came he not home tonight?°

Benvolio Not to his father's. I spoke with his man.

Mercutio Why, that same pale hardhearted wench, that Rosaline,
Torments him so, that he will sure run mad.

Benvolio Tybalt, the kinsman of old Capulet,
Hath sent a letter to his father's house.

Mercutio A challenge, on my life.

Benvolio Romeo will answer it.°

Mercutio Any man that can write may answer a letter.

Benvolio Nay, he will answer the letter's master, how° he dares, being dared.°

Mercutio Alas poor Romeo, he is already dead: stabbed with a white wench's black eye, run through the ear with a love song; the very pin° of his heart cleft with the blind bow-boy's butt-shaft.° And is he a man to encounter Tybalt?

Benvolio Why, what° is Tybalt?

Mercutio More than Prince of Cats, I can tell you. O he's the courageous captain of compliments.° He fights as you sing pricksong:° keeps time, distance, and proportion. He rests his minim rests,° one, two, and the third in your bosom. The very butcher of a silk button,° a duelist, a duelist! A gentleman of the very first house,° of the first and second cause.° Ah the immortal *passado!*° The *punto reverso!*° The hay!°

Benvolio The what?

Mercutio The pox of° such antic,° lisping, affecting fantasticoes,° these new tuners of accent! "By Jesu, a very good

can

last night

accept the challenge

as

challenged

bull's eye (of target)

Cupid's practice (unbarbed) arrow

what a thing (derisive)

niceties (of dueling)

sing from printed music

i.e., he is technically briliant

i.e., on an opponent's shirt

highest rank grounds for duel

lunge backhanded stroke thrust home (dueling terms)

A plague on grotesque

fops

Scene iv

**1-9** The two young men are restless. The incomplete verse-line (2) shows that Mercutio's two questions are separated by a pause. Benvolio replies in two short phrases, the second only supporting the first.

In most productions, they meet as in a street among other Montagues and walk up and down, or sit around drinking or playing idly at some game. The change of subject at line 6 shows that Benvolio has been deeply worried from the beginning. With Mercutio's short response (l. 8), there is an abrupt and serious silence; at this point, verse gives way to prose which allows a more casual tone as if they recognize that all they can do is wait to see what happens.

**10-33** Mercutio's answer to uncertainty and danger is to joke and then speak fantastically, in scorn of his friend. He imagines the lovesick Romeo to be killed three times over and the impetuous Tybalt to be absurdly intent on swordmanship. Rhythm is sustained by threefold descriptions, repetitions, and short exclamations. Mercutio becomes so caught up in his fantasies that he speaks for Tybalt (ll. 27-28) and then continues as if he were an old fool mocking young men. He ends with what is probably an allusion to syphilis, or the bone-ache.

So much energy is in Mercutio's mockery that he may seem to be speaking in order to cover up a genuine worry about Romeo or a love for him that resents his involvement with Rosaline; alternatively, he may be expressing an envy of Romeo or of Tybalt's reputation for swordsmanship.

Most Mercutios accompany their words with physical impersonations; some half-scare Benvolio with swordplay and end with arms around him as if supporting the weakness of old age. Or Mercutio may pretend to talk to a third person and point to Benvolio as one of the "fashionmongers." Much depends on Benvolio's reactions: he can laugh easily, or be partly puzzled, or he may remain apprehensive (see note, lines 1-9), which would explain why he is the first to see Romeo's silent entry.

blade! A very tall° man! A very good whore!" Why, is not this a lamentable thing, grandsir, that we should be thus afflicted with these strange flies, these fashionmongers, these pardon-me's,° who stand° so much on the new form° that they cannot sit at ease on the old bench? O their bones,° their bones!

*Enter* ROMEO.

BENVOLIO Here comes Romeo, here comes Romeo!

MERCUTIO Without his roe,° like a dried herring. O flesh, flesh, how art thou fishified!° Now is he for the numbers° that Petrarch flowed in. Laura, to° his lady, was a kitchen wench—marry, she had a better love to be-rhyme her—Dido a dowdy,° Cleopatra a gypsy, Helen and Hero hildings° and harlots, Thisbe a gray eye or so, but not to the purpose.—Signior Romeo, *bon jour*.° There's a French salutation to your French slop.° You gave us the counterfeit fairly last night.

ROMEO Good morrow to you both. What counterfeit did I give you?

MERCUTIO The slip° sir, the slip. Can you not conceive?

ROMEO Pardon good Mercutio. My business was great;° and in such a case as mine a man may strain courtesy.

MERCUTIO That's as much as to say, such a case° as yours constrains a man to bow in the hams.

ROMEO Meaning, to curtsy.°

MERCUTIO Thou hast most kindly° hit it.°

ROMEO A most courteous exposition.

MERCUTIO Nay, I am the very pink° of courtesy.

ROMEO Pink for flower.

MERCUTIO Right.

ROMEO Why then is my pump well flowered.°

MERCUTIO Sure wit. Follow me this jest now, till thou hast worn out thy pump, that when the single sole of it is worn, the jest may remain, after the wearing, solely singular.°

brave

polite, affected talkers

insist code of manners

(pun on Fr. *bon*)

gutless/without his dear (pun: *roe* = deer)

made cold, bloodless verses

compared with

slut

broken down jades

good day

loose breeches

escape/counterfeit coin

(play on conceive=become *great* with child)

circumstance/clothes

bow (pun on *courtesy*, line 46)

exactly/pleasantly hit on it

perfection* (*flower* was the usual word in the phrase)

my shoe is well pinked, i.e., pierced for decoration

uniquely unique (pun on *soul* surviving the *worn* body)

**34-41** Mercutio tries to get Romeo to respond by mocking him. All his references are to ill-starred lovers: Petrarch wrote his sonnets to the Laura he had first seen in a church—some scholars think she never existed; Dido committed suicide when Aeneas left her, and so did Cleopatra and Thisbe after the suicides of their lovers; Hero killed herself after Leander was drowned; the Trojan war was fought after the rape of Menelaus' wife, Helen. Finally, receiving no response, Mercutio, mimicking the "fantasticoes" (see ll. 26-7), greets Romeo directly.

Again Mercutio's mockery seems too pressured to be simple verbal sport: he may try to rouse Romeo so that he can tease him further; or the outpouring of words may be an expression of sheer pleasure in his company.

**42-61** Romeo breaks his silence with simple politeness but then joins Mercutio in wordplay, at first with mock courtesy, then with increasing sharpness and attack. At lines 56-58, Mercutio tries to outpace him, but Romeo caps his punning with a single, fluent, tightly packed line. When Mercutio pretends to be defeated, Romeo presses home his advantage. The lively words and laughter are usually matched with physical mockery and mimicry. At line 60, Mercutio either goes to sit down or moves the silent Benvolio (who may pretend to be frightened) between himself and Romeo.

ROMEO O single-soled° jest, solely singular for the singleness!°

MERCUTIO Come between° us, good Benvolio! My wits faints.

ROMEO Swits° and spurs, swits and spurs; or I'll cry a match.°

MERCUTIO Nay, if our wits run the wild-goose chase,° I am done;° for thou hast more of the wild goose in one of thy wits than I am sure I have in my whole five. Was I with you there for the goose?°

ROMEO Thou wast never with me for any thing when thou wast not there for the goose.°

MERCUTIO I will bite thee by the ear° for that jest.

ROMEO Nay good goose, bite not.°

MERCUTIO Thy wit is a very bitter sweeting;° it is a most sharp sauce.°

ROMEO And is it not, then, well served in to a sweet goose?°

MERCUTIO O here's a wit of cheveril,° that stretches from an inch narrow to an ell broad!°

ROMEO I stretch it out for that word "broad," which added to the goose, proves thee far and wide a broad° goose.

MERCUTIO Why is not this better now than groaning for love? Now art thou sociable, now art thou Romeo; now art thou what thou art, by art as well as by nature. For this driveling love is like a great natural° that runs lolling° up and down to hide his bauble in a hole.°

BENVOLIO Stop there, stop there.

MERCUTIO Thou desirest me to stop in my tale against the hair.°

BENVOLIO Thou wouldst else have made thy tale large.°

MERCUTIO O thou art deceived! I would have made it° short; for I was come to the whole depth of my tale, and meant indeed to occupy° the argument no longer.

ROMEO Here's goodly gear!°

*Enter* NURSE *and her man,* [PETER.]

thin, weak silliness

part

whips (play on *wits*) victory

follow-the-leader

finished

did I outwit you with "the goose"

whore/fool

i.e., as mark of affection

spare me (proverbial)

sour-sweet apple (pun on *bite*)

applesauce (for goose)/sharp rebuke

dear fool (Mercutio)

kid leather

forty-five inches wide

obvious/gross

born idiot with tongue hanging out

i.e., to copulate

against my inclination (puns on *there*, and on pubic *hair*)

indecent/lengthy

tail (i.e., penis)

deal with/copulate with

business

**62-81** When Mercutio returns to the combat of wit, the tone is more "sociable": see "our wits" and "Was I with you..." and the longer phrasing of lines 66-67. They probably sit down together as the talk becomes familiarly bawdy. When Mercutio claims a victory in regaining Romeo from love (ll. 77-9), he follows this with more outrageous sexual innuendo than before that devalues the act and effects of sexual encounter (ll. 79-81).

**82-7** Mercutio has probably gone too far for Romeo. When Benvolio tries to intervene, he only encourages Mercutio to press on with evident pleasure, now using Benvolio as the stimulus for his humor and pretending to ignore Romeo.

Romeo has probably walked away and so sees the nurse first.

**88-95** The nurse enters in some style and stops as she sees the young men. They usually laugh at her openly. Peter has to catch up while she prepares herself like a fine lady for the encounter. Romeo will

A sail, a sail!

MERCUTIO Two, two! A shirt and a smock.°

NURSE Peter!

PETER Anon.

NURSE My fan, Peter.

MERCUTIO Good Peter, to hide her face; for her fan's the fairer face.

NURSE God ye good morrow,° gentlemen.

MERCUTIO God ye good-den,° fair gentlewoman.

NURSE Is it good-den?

MERCUTIO 'Tis no less, I tell ye; for the bawdy hand° of the dial is now upon the prick° of noon.

NURSE Out upon you! What a man° are you!

ROMEO One, gentlewoman, that God hath made for himself to mar.

NURSE By my troth, it is well said: "For himself to mar," quoth 'a!° Gentlemen, can any of you tell me where I may find the young Romeo?

ROMEO I can tell you. But young Romeo will be older when you have found him than he was when you sought him. I am the youngest° of that name, for fault of a worse.°

NURSE You say well.

MERCUTIO Yea, is the worst well? Very well took,° i' faith! Wisely, wisely!

NURSE If you be he sir, I desire some confidence° with you.

BENVOLIO She will endite° him to some supper.

MERCUTIO A bawd,° a bawd, a bawd! So ho!°

ROMEO What hast thou found?

MERCUTIO No hare° sir; unless a hare, sir, in a lenten° pie, that is something stale and hoar° ere it be spent.

[*He walks by them and sings.*]

recognize Juliet's nurse and stand aside, ready to receive a message.

a man and a woman

morning

good-evening (afternoon)

**97-106** Mercutio answers with unnecessary and undeserved compliment and, then, shocks the nurse with a bawdy joke. At line 102, Romeo steps in to reassure the nurse and prevent her leaving: this involves a shrewd criticism of his friend which probably adds to Mercutio's amusement, but for the moment he is quiet and the nurse can put her question. The nurse is in some difficulty and so flustered between her fine airs and the bawdy talk that she has not recognized Romeo whom she knew the night before.

i.e., hour (whore) hand

point/penis

what kind of man

he

**107-09** Romeo may speak circuitously because he is aware of Mercutio watching closely.

i.e., the only one (parodying "for want of a better")

understood

private talk (perhaps error for conference)

invite

procuress (huntsman's cry)

(pun on "whore") meatless

moldy (pun on "whore," or *stale*)

**113-28** The nurse pays no attention to Mercutio now and tries to draw Romeo aside. Benvolio is the first to express his amazement and then Mercutio cries out like a huntsman, amazed and delighted, thinking that, after all, Romeo has been deceiving them and has treated sex as a mere convenience. Mercutio crows with pleasure and puts on an absurd act, like a one-man carnival. He pretends the nurse is the whore, again taking a flight of fantasy and turning all to grotesque absurdity. His brief word with Romeo (l. 125) is to let him know that all this is an act put on so that they can leave him alone to hear from his

An old hare hoar,°
And an old hare hoar,
  Is very good meat° in Lent.
But a hare that is hoar
Is too much for a score,°
When it hoars ere it be spent.°

Romeo, will you come to your father's? We'll to dinner there.

ROMEO I will follow you.

MERCUTIO Farewell ancient lady, farewell! [*Sings.*] "Lady, lady, lady."° *Exeunt* [MERCUTIO *and* BENVOLIO.]

NURSE I pray you sir, what saucy merchant° was this that was so full of his ropery?°

ROMEO A gentleman, Nurse, that loves to hear himself talk, and will speak more in a minute than he will stand to° in a month.

NURSE And a'° speak anything against me, I'll take him down,° and 'a were lustier than he is, and twenty such Jacks; and if I cannot, I'll find those that shall. Scurvy knave! I am none of his flirt-gills;° I am none of his skainsmates.° [*To* PETER.] And thou must stand by too, and suffer every knave to use° me at his pleasure!

PETER I saw no man use you at his pleasure. If I had, my weapon° should quickly have been out, I warrant you. I dare draw as soon as another man, if I see occasion in a good quarrel, and the law on my side.

NURSE Now, afore God, I am so vexed that every part about me quivers. Scurvy knave! Pray you sir, a word:—and, as I told you, my young lady bid me inquire you out. What she bid me say, I will keep to myself. But first let me tell ye, if ye should lead her in a fool's paradise,° as they say, it were a very gross kind of behavior, as they say; for the gentlewoman is young, and therefore if you should deal double° with her, truly it were an ill thing to be off'red to any gentlewoman, and very weak° dealing.

ROMEO Nurse, commend me to thy lady and mistress. I protest° unto thee—

grey-white

food/whore

not worth paying for

eaten/exhausted

(refrain of the ballad, "Chaste Susanna")

insolent fellow

knavery

abide by

he humble him (with unwitting sexual innuendo)

loose women fellow cut-throats

(unwitting sexual pun)

sword/penis

i.e., seduce her

deceitfully

feeble, contemptible

declare

whore. He makes his exit with mocking courtesy to the nurse and the refrain of a ballad of chaste love.

In all this the actor has ample opportunity for catcalls, whistles, obscene gestures, mock refinement, wolf-cries, and so forth; usually Mercutio dances offstage, still singing loudly or laughing. But under the obvious hilarity, there can be sense of desperation that pushes the horseplay too far; the comedy, for all its high spirits, is destructive.

**129-38** The nurse is speechless at first, but finds her tongue when Mercutio leaves. Her righteous indignation is accentuated by contrast with Romeo's reassuring, careful answer. At line 137, she usually turns in violent anger on the astonished Peter, who has not said or done a thing during the whole encounter.

**139-42** Peter's reply is reminiscent of the boasting talk of Gregory and Sampson, two other Capulet servants, in the first scene of the play; for an audience it may be a reminder of the unthinking violence that has been bred between the two houses and of the brutality towards women that it has encouraged.

**143-62** With obvious effort, the nurse starts to deliver her message, drawing Romeo away from Peter. As soon as they are alone, however, she speaks her own mind first. This moment of sincere concern is all the more effective by contrast with the noisy preparation for it.

As the nurse grows more involved, Romeo gently and earnestly breaks in with his message. By line 159, he has decided to say as little as possible, as clearly as he can. Again, all is quiet as he tells the plan on which so much depends and which is so against the pressures of the ancient family feud. A return to verse heightens an impression of renewed purpose.

NURSE Good heart, and i' faith, I will tell her as much. Lord, Lord, she will be a joyful woman.

ROMEO What wilt thou tell her, Nurse? Thou dost not mark me.

NURSE I will tell her sir, that you do protest;° which, as I take it, is a gentlemanlike offer.

ROMEO Bid her devise
Some means to come to shrift° this afternoon;
And there she shall at Friar Lawrence' cell
Be shrived° and married. Here is for thy pains. [*Gives money.*]

NURSE No truly, sir; not a penny.

ROMEO Go to, I say you shall.

NURSE This afternoon sir? Well, she shall be there.

ROMEO And stay good Nurse, behind the abbey wall.
Within this hour my man shall be with thee
And bring thee cords made like a tackled stair,°
Which to the high topgallant° of my joy
Must be my convoy° in the secret night.
Farewell. Be trusty, and I'll quit° thy pains.
Farewell. Commend me to thy mistress.

NURSE Now God in heaven bless thee! Hark you sir.

ROMEO What say'st thou my dear Nurse?

NURSE Is your man secret? Did you ne'er hear say,
Two may keep counsel, putting one away?

ROMEO I warrant thee my man's as true as steel.

NURSE Well sir, my mistress is the sweetest lady. Lord, Lord, when 'twas a little prating thing . . . O there is a nobleman in town, one Paris, that would fain lay knife aboard;° but she, good soul, had as lieve° see a toad, a very toad, as see him. I anger her sometimes, and tell her that Paris is the properer° man; but I'll warrant you, when I say so, she looks as pale as any clout° in the versal° world. Doth not rosemary and Romeo begin both with a letter?°

ROMEO Ay Nurse; what of that? Both with an *R*.

The nurse says nothing now, taking it all in. In offering money, Romeo makes clear that he knows his message has been received and that they are ready to part.

vow (love)

confession

absolved

**163-65** By silently accepting the money, after having refused it, the nurse shows her connivance in Romeo's plan and her own cunning, nicety, or self-deception, whichever suits best with the actress's interpretation of the role.

**166-72** As Romeo elaborates his plan he is drawn into lyricism and, then at line 171, returns briskly to his business and departure. All this can be instinctive while the need for action takes over in his mind, or it can show an increasing awareness that he cannot expect anyone else to understand the nature of his feelings.

rope ladder
peak (platform at head of top mast)
conveyance
repay

**173-91** The nurse calls Romeo back as he is leaving. She is so pleased with events (and herself) that she must show her ability to be "trusty" (see line 171) and her awareness of the difficulties of what is planned (ll. 175-6). Romeo's "my dear Nurse" suggests that he now feels closer to her. Much of what he hears must please him, but he says little and leaves quickly, intent on his business.

The nurse usually plays up the drama, as she sees it, confiding to Romeo behind her fan, chuckling at the "prating thing," mimicking Juliet's response to a "toad," and so on. With "mocker" she is waggish, believing she shares an intimate joke.

lay claim to her (by bringing knife to table)/assault her
as soon

more handsome

cloth, rag universal (illiterate)
the same letter

NURSE Ah mocker, that's the dog's name.° *R* is for the . . . No: I know it begins with some other letter; and she hath the prettiest sententious° of it, of you and rosemary, that it would do you good to hear it.

ROMEO Commend me to thy lady. [*Exit* ROMEO.]

NURSE Ay, a thousand times. Peter!

PETER Anon.

NURSE Before, and apace. *Exit* [*after* PETER.]

Scene v *Enter* JULIET.

JULIET The clock struck nine when I did send the nurse;
In half an hour she promised to return.
Perchance she cannot meet him. That's not so.
O she is lame! Love's heralds should be thoughts,
Which ten times faster glides than the sun's beams
Driving back shadows over low'ring hills.
Therefore do nimble-pinioned° doves° draw Love,
And therefore hath the wind-swift Cupid wings.
Now is the sun upon the highmost hill°
Of this day's journey, and from nine till twelve
Is three long hours; yet she is not come.
Had she affections and warm youthful blood,
She would be as swift in motion as a ball;
My words would bandy° her to my sweet love,
And his to me.
But old folks, many feign as they were dead,
Unwieldy, slow, heavy, and pale as lead.°

*Enter* NURSE [*and* PETER.]

O God, she comes! O honey Nurse, what news?
Hast thou met with him? Send thy man away.

NURSE Peter, stay at the gate.° [*Exit* PETER.]

(*R* sounds like a growl)

(mistake for "sentence" = saying)

**192-94** The nurse, to her surprise, finds that Romeo has gone. She suddenly turns on Peter, either in anger or sharing Romeo's sense of urgency. Peter is usually asleep, or otherwise occupied. As she exerts her authority, there is opportunity for a quick comic exit.

Scene v

**1-17** Juliet usually runs on-stage or is first seen looking out from the balcony above the stage. She is agitated and impatient, yet tries to be reasonable. She is also delighted and excited, and this is expressed by imagery involving flight and light and the sky, and also a game. Rhythms express the same feelings, for example, with the two phrases of line 4, the second growing out of the first and leading to the extended description and longer phrasing of lines 5-6. The short line 15 suggests a silence of unspoken anticipation following the simple naming of her "sweet love."

swift winged (sacred to Venus, they *draw* her chariot)

i.e., it is midday

strike to and fro (as in tennis)

i.e., many old people move as if they were almost dead

**18-34** Juliet quickly greets the nurse on her entry. The command to Peter is an opportunity for the clown to repeat and develop whatever comic business he had used on his previous exit and so height-

wait at the entrance

JULIET Now good sweet Nurse—O Lord, why lookest thou sad?
Though news be sad, yet tell them merrily;
If good, thou shamest the music of sweet news
By playing it to me with so sour a face.

NURSE I am aweary, give me leave° awhile.
Fie, how my bones ache! What a jaunce° have I!

JULIET I would thou hadst my bones, and I thy news.
Nay come, I pray thee speak. Good, good Nurse, speak.

NURSE Jesu, what haste! Can you not stay° awhile?
Do you not see that I am out of breath?

JULIET How art thou out of breath, when thou hast breath
To say to me that thou art out of breath?
The excuse that thou dost make in this delay
Is longer than the tale thou dost excuse.
Is thy news good or bad? Answer to that.
Say either, and I'll stay the circumstance.°
Let me be satisfied, is't good or bad?

NURSE Well, you have made a simple° choice; you know not how to choose a man. Romeo? No, not he. Though his face be better than any man's, yet his leg excels all men's; and for a hand and a foot, and a body, though they be not to be talked on,° yet they are past compare. He is not the flower of courtesy, but I'll warrant him, as gentle as a lamb. Go thy ways, wench; serve God. What, have you dined at home?

JULIET No, no. But all this did I know before.
What says he of our marriage, what of that?

NURSE Lord, how my head aches! What a head have I!
It beats as it would fall in twenty pieces.
My back—a' t'other side—ah, my back, my back!
Beshrew° your heart for sending me about
To catch my death with jauncing° up and down.

JULIET I' faith I am sorry that thou art not well.
Sweet, sweet, sweet Nurse, tell me, what says my love?

NURSE Your love says, like an honest° gentleman, and a courteous, and a kind, and a handsome, and I warrant, a virtuous—Where is your mother?

en Juliet's impatience and the audience's expectation.

Juliet will wait until Peter is gone and then run to the nurse, only to realize that her confidante stands still and uncommunicative. The nurse sits at line 25 and can either tease Juliet by her delay or else be truly "out of breath"; possibly, now that she is home, she may be apprehensive about her part in the elopement. Whichever way it is played, the nurse's delay accentuates Juliet's dependence on her and points up her unreflecting eagerness to be with Romeo.

let me alone

jaunt, weary journey

Juliet's reactions in this scene can be played in different ways. Ellen Terry's *Memoirs* (1932) explains that: "Tradition said that Juliet must go on coquetting and clicking over the Nurse to get the news of Romeo out of her. Tradition said that Juliet must give imitations of the Nurse on the line, 'Where's your mother' (60), in order to get that cheap reward, 'a safe laugh.' I felt that it was wrong. I felt that Juliet was angry with the Nurse. Each time she delayed in answering I lost my temper, with genuine passion. At 'Where's your mother?' I spoke with indignation, rage and tears." The scene reads easily and has unfailing interest when performed, but it is a difficult one for the actress to judge rightly: Juliet can be too childish, too cross, indignant, or impatient; she may also appear wholly in command through an inner assurance that the nurse fails to see, and so all the "coil" is in the old woman's complaints and petty artifices.

wait

wait for details

foolish

not worth mentioning

**35** This question is crucial to Juliet. She may say it slowly and pointedly, which will tend to accentuate her anticipation of happiness, or she may speak very quickly, as if afraid of the answer.

**38-46** The nurse probably speaks slowly—irritatingly so for Juliet—while studying her listener's face and sometimes falling silent as if caught in her own thoughts: the change to prose gives freedom for this. Her question at line 44 (like the one later at line 56) may arise from genuine uneasiness, but Juliet does not notice this.

confound

traipsing

**49** Juliet tries to humor the nurse by rubbing her back.

**52-56** As soon as Juliet expresses concern for her aches, the nurse begins to tell her news. If Juliet is played as a very young girl of fourteen (as I.ii requires), she may now hug and kiss the nurse, as a little child might do in relief and gratification; but all this must stop after the first three words of line 54

honorable

JULIET Where is my mother? Why she is within.
Where should she be? How oddly thou repliest!
"Your love says, like an honest gentleman,
'Where is your mother?'"

NURSE O God's Lady dear!
Are you so hot? Marry come up,° I trow.°
Is this the poultice for my aching bones?
Henceforward do your messages yourself.

JULIET Here's such a coil!° Come, what says Romeo?

NURSE Have you got leave to go to shrift° today?

JULIET I have.

NURSE Then hie° you hence to Friar Lawrence' cell:
There stays a husband to make you a wife.
Now comes the wanton blood up in your cheeks:
They'll be in scarlet straight° at any news.
Hie you to church. I must another way,
To fetch a ladder, by the which your love
Must climb a bird's nest° soon when it is dark.
I am the drudge, and toil in° your delight;
But you shall bear the burden° soon at night.
Go. I'll to dinner. Hie you to the cell.

JULIET Hie to high fortune! Honest Nurse, farewell. *Exeunt.*

Scene vi *Enter* FRIAR LAWRENCE *and* ROMEO.

FRIAR So smile the heavens° upon this holy act
That afterhours with sorrow chide us not.

ROMEO Amen, amen! But come what sorrow can,°
It cannot countervail° the exchange of joy°
That one short minute gives me in her sight.
Do thou but close our hands with holy words,
Then love-devouring Death do what he dare:
It is enough I may but call her mine.

when Juliet becomes still and perhaps tense. Maddenly for her listener, the nurse then starts speaking of her own opinions; often this is done intentionally in order to get more attention but, if so, the ruse is apt to be counterproductive.

come off it to be sure

fuss

confession

haste

straightway

i.e., Juliet's room (*bird*=maiden)

for

do the work/bear the weight of your lover

**57-77** Some Juliets lose patience here; others mock the nurse. When the nurse threatens to say nothing more (l. 63), Juliet recognizes either that she has been teased or that she herself has made matters worse. A change of tone and a simple question get a direct answer, although in the form of another question. Juliet's "I have" is submissive in anticipation, but the final, long-awaited news at line 68 leaves her, after so many eager words, wholly silent and lost in her own thoughts. She will probably remain silent and unmoving as the nurse repeats and completes her instructions and her complaints. Only the brisk commands of line 76 cause Juliet to speak and to leave the stage.

The nurse's allusions to the bridal night are at first (ll. 72-3) both provocative and gently sympathetic; later (l. 75) she becomes more direct and almost blunt. The actress must choose, carefully, how these lines are spoken: they can be responsive and caring or they can express a more selfish relish for Juliet's predicament.

With the wordplay on "hie" and "high," in one brief ecstatic phrase, Juliet commits herself to her love and (for the audience) to her tragic fate. She usually stops only to kiss the nurse and then runs offstage, leaving the nurse to make a separate, slower exit.

## Scene vi

may the heavens so smile

all possible sorrow

equal mutual joy

**1-8** The friar's first lines are both a prayer and an expression of fear for the future. He is recalled to immediate business by Romeo's impulsive words and rhythms. Line 7 can suggest that Romeo is acting defiance of a fear of some bitter "consequence" (I.iv.106-7) which he cannot erase from his mind. Alternatively, and more simply, it may be, like line 3, a straightforward or, even, brash response to the friar's fears.

FRIAR These violent delights have violent ends
And in their triumph die, like fire and powder,°
Which, as they kiss, consume. The sweetest honey
Is loathsome in his own deliciousness,
And in the taste confounds° the appetite.
Therefore love moderately: long love doth so.
Too swift arrives as tardy as too slow.

*Enter* JULIET.

Here comes the lady. O so light a foot
Will ne'er wear out the everlasting flint.°
A lover may bestride the gossamers,
That idles in the wanton° summer air,
And yet not fall: so light is vanity.°

JULIET Good even to my ghostly° confessor.

FRIAR Romeo shall thank thee, daughter, for us both.

JULIET As much to him, else is his thanks too much.

ROMEO Ah Juliet, if the measure of thy joy
Be heaped like mine, and that thy skill be more
To blazon it,° then sweeten with thy breath
This neighbor air, and let rich music's tongue°
Unfold the imagined happiness that both
Receive in either by this dear encounter.

JULIET Conceit, more rich in matter than in words,
Brags of his substance, not of ornament.°
They are but beggars that can count their worth;
But my true love is grown to such excess°
I cannot sum up sum° of half my wealth.

FRIAR Come, come with me, and we will make short work;
For, by your leaves, you shall not stay alone,
Till Holy Church incorporate two in one. [*Exeunt.*]

gunpowder

destroys

Juliet, alight with love, treads less firmly than waterdrops, which are said to wear away the hardest stone

capricious

i.e., vanity of human desires

spiritual

and if you are better able to proclaim it

i.e., your voice

the mind, fuller in experience than talk, takes pride in life and not in art

has received such interest

give the total

**9-15** The friar now covers up any particular fears he may have had with more general exhortations against indulging sexual passions. Romeo has no answer; perhaps the friar's earnestness allows him no opportunity for one.

**16-20** The First Quarto has a stage direction that reads like a description of an early performance: "Enter Juliet somewhat fast, and embraceth Romeo." The friar stands aside, speaking his thoughts: that Juliet is too delicate to endure the hardness of life. This response implies both instinctive tenderness and fear for what he can foresee. The change of tone from the moralizing of lines 9-15 (clinched by a couplet) is marked in performance, giving a moment when the dramatic action seems to stand still as the lovers are silent in their embrace, and as the audience is free to respond as it wishes to the friar's choric comment.

**22** When Juliet belatedly greets him, the friar, for once, has nothing to say. He gently and happily accepts that the lovers' obvious delight in each other excludes almost every other thought.

**23-34** After Juliet speaks for the first time, Shakespeare has given each of the lovers a speech of leaping imagery and sustained rhythms that expresses such pleasure that neither is able to give adequate response, even with these rich words. Then they stand back, gazing into each other's eyes, as their happiness seems to overwhelm and silence each of them in turn.

**35-37** At the end of this Act, the friar no longer debates what he or the lovers should do. His speed can have a comic effect, because he has hitherto counseled slowness and because he may seem to be suddenly afraid of the consequences of leaving the two young lovers alone. But his change of tactic can also be affecting, as he recognizes the strength of their feelings and as the lovers stand together, silent, and ready for the religious ceremony. Romeo and Juliet walk silently to their wedding with a new solemnity or as in a dream.

How they leave the stage is an important element in each characterization. By the friar's words and his need to wait for them, Shakespeare has directed attention on them unreservedly, and their silent response is wide open for individual interpretation. In Zeffirelli's Old Vic production, "Romeo walked

# ACT III

Scene i *Enter* MERCUTIO, BENVOLIO, *and* MEN.

BENVOLIO I pray thee good Mercutio, let's retire.
The day is hot, the Capels° are abroad,
And if we meet, we shall not 'scape a brawl,
For now these hot days, is the mad blood stirring.

MERCUTIO Thou art like one of those fellows that when he enters the confines of a tavern, claps° me his sword upon the table, and says, "God send me no need of thee!";° and by the operation of the second cup, draws him on the drawer,° when indeed there is no need.

BENVOLIO Am I° like such a fellow?

MERCUTIO Come, come, thou art as hot a Jack in thy mood° as any in Italy; and as soon moved to be moody,° and as soon moody to be moved.°

BENVOLIO And what to?

MERCUTIO Nay, and there were two° such, we should have none shortly, for one would kill the other. Thou! Why, thou wilt quarrel with a man that hath a hair more or a hair less in his beard than thou hast. Thou wilt quarrel with a man for cracking nuts, having no other reason but because thou hast hazel eyes. What eye, but such an eye,° would spy out such a quarrel? Thy head is as full of quarrels as an egg is full of meat; and yet thy head hath been beaten as addle° as an egg for quarreling. Thou hast quarrelled with a man for coughing in the street, because he hath awakened thy dog that hath lain asleep in the sun. Didst thou not fall out with a tailor for wearing his new doublet° before Easter?° With another for tying his new shoes with old riband?° And yet thou wilt tutor me from quarreling!

backwards so that he continued to face Juliet who was supported on the Friar's arm: Romeo was 'bewitched by the charm of looks' (II.Chorus 6), rapt in 'the imagined happiness that both receive in either by this dear encounter' (II.vi. 28-29)" (*Shakespeare Survey*, 1962). The effect was both affecting and absurd.

## ACT III. Scene i

Capulets

**1** The stage is crowded for the first time since the Ball scene (I.v). Here and at line 31, Shakespeare has directed supernumeraries to come on-stage without specifying what they should do. Benvolio's first speech suggests that they should prowl, warily and wearily, around the stage.

thrusts down

i.e., daring others to be offensive

draws his sword on the waiter

**1-31** Benvolio draws Mercutio aside, speaking earnestly. This provokes Mercutio to mock his prudence by branding him as the opposite sort of man, a quarreler. The energy of this episode derives wholly from Mercutio's fantasy that overrides his friend's justifiable incredulity as well as his caution. Although Mercutio may lounge at his ease as he talks, he clearly relishes the thought of quarreling. He attracts attention from everyone else on-stage and, at length, criticism and a sober warning from Benvolio (ll. 28-30). He answers this with a simple pun and, presumably, laughter.

(implying "you are"; see line 28)

temper

provoked to be angry

angry to be provoked

(pun on *to*, line 14)

(pun on *I*)

rotten

close-fitting jacket

(occasion for wearing new clothing)

ribbon

BENVOLIO And I were so apt to quarrel as thou art, any man should buy the fee simple° of my life for an hour and a quarter.°

MERCUTIO The fee simple? O simple!°

*Enter* TYBALT *and others.*

BENVOLIO By my head, here comes the Capulets.

MERCUTIO By my heel, I care not.

TYBALT Follow me close, for I will speak to them.
Gentlemen, good-den;° a word with one of you.

MERCUTIO And but° one word with one of us? Couple it with something; make it a word and a blow.

TYBALT You shall find me apt enough to that sir, and you will give me occasion.°

MERCUTIO Could you not take some occasion without giving?

TYBALT Mercutio, thou consortest° with Romeo.

MERCUTIO Consort?° What, dost thou make us minstrels?° And thou make minstrels of us, look to hear nothing but discords. Here's my fiddlestick;° here's that shall make you dance. Zounds,° consort!

BENVOLIO We talk here in the public haunt° of men.
Either withdraw unto some private place,
Or reason coldly° of your grievances,
Or else depart.° Here all eyes gaze on us.

MERCUTIO Men's eyes were made to look, and let them gaze.
I will not budge for no man's pleasure, I.

*Enter* ROMEO.

TYBALT Well, peace be with you sir. Here comes my man.

MERCUTIO But I'll be hanged sir, if he wear your livery.°
Marry,° go before to field,° he'll be your follower!°
Your worship in that sense may call him man.°

absolute possession
i.e., he would be dead before that time was passed
stupid

**31-35** Tybalt's entry at the head of a group, or gang, of Capulets brings a sudden silence as the Montagues draw together, ready for trouble. By ostentatiously assuming indifference, Mercutio challenges Tybalt. After curtly ordering the Capulets to follow him, Tybalt moves across stage. He is silent until close enough to speak with studied politeness to the Montagues.

good-evening (afternoon)

only

**36-45** Closely watched by everyone else (see line 49), Mercutio and Tybalt bandy polite insults. As Tybalt names his quarry, Mercutio picks on a somewhat pompous word and makes a quarrel of that: as his talk becomes more fantastic, he reaches for his sword.

excuse

associate

harmonize (in music) hired musicians (i.e., servants)

i.e., sword

by God's wounds

resort

**46-51** Benvolio goes to Mercutio's side and earnestly reasons with him. They are still watched by everyone. Mercutio stands his ground, making it impossible for Tybalt to withdraw without loss of face. By now Mercutio seems wholly in charge, but when Romeo enters Tybalt turns to him, as does everyone else.

discuss calmly

part

servant's uniform (play on *man* = servant)
indeed place for dueling
pursuer/retainer
man of honor, no coward

**52-68** Coming from the marriage ceremony, Romeo finds everyone looking at him. He is silent, but Mercutio keeps up a running commentary until Tybalt confronts Romeo. As Tybalt's hand goes to his sword, the confrontation becomes still more critical. Romeo answers carefully, thinking far more than he can say. By denying the charge of "villain," he shows

TYBALT Romeo, the love I bear thee can afford
No better term than this: thou art a villain.

ROMEO Tybalt, the reason that I have to love thee
Doth much excuse the appertaining° rage
To such a greeting. Villain am I none.
Therefore farewell; I see thou knowest me not.

TYBALT Boy, this shall not excuse the injuries
That thou hast done me; therefore turn and draw.

ROMEO I do protest I never injured thee,
But love thee better than thou canst devise,°
Till thou shalt know the reason of my love.
And so, good Capulet, which name I tender°
As dearly as mine own, be satisfied.

MERCUTIO O calm, dishonourable, vile submission!
*Alla stoccata*° carries it away. [*Draws.*]
Tybalt, you ratcatcher, will you walk?°

TYBALT What wouldst thou have with me?

MERCUTIO Good King of Cats, nothing but one of your nine lives. That I mean to make bold withal,° and as you shall use me hereafter, dry-beat° the rest of the eight. Will you pluck your sword out of his pilcher by the ears?° Make haste, lest mine be about your ears ere it be out.

TYBALT I am for you. [*Draws.*]

ROMEO Gentle Mercutio, put thy rapier up.

MERCUTIO Come sir, your *passado*!° [*They fight.*]

ROMEO Draw BENVOLIO; beat down their weapons.
Gentlemen, for shame, forbear this outrage!
Tybalt! Mercutio! The prince expressly hath
Forbid this bandying° in Verona streets.
Hold Tybalt! Good Mercutio!

[TYBALT *under* ROMEO's *arm thrusts* MERCUTIO *in,*° *and flies.*]

MERCUTIO I am hurt.
A plague a'° both your houses! I am sped.°
Is he gone and hath nothing?°

he knows what is at stake, even as he turns away from his accuser.

appropriate

Rapidly, Tybalt adds the insult of "Boy" and calls for a fight. The crowd begin to make a circle marking the space for a duel; some may begin to jeer or shout out support for one side or the other. In response, Romeo now goes much further, speaking of "love" for his enemy and for the very name of Capulet; he speaks with strong emotion, as he thinks of his bride whom he has just left (ll. 67-8). Quiet and persistent, he is feeling his way into a new self and a new social reality; alone in this excited mob, he is "calm" (see l. 69) as he breaks traditional mores and taboos.

imagine

value

at the thrust (dueling term) wins the day

make a move

**69-78** An uncomprehending and outraged Mercutio challenges Tybalt and, as his adversary turns to him, his fantasy is again engaged in a demeaning and brutal mockery that he adds to the confrontation. With four brief words (l. 78), both swords are out and, with quick inevitability, everyone falls silent and tense, ready for the fight.

make free with (i.e., take)

thrash

drag your sword out of its coat (contemptuous)

**79-85** Romeo appeals first to his friend, who pointedly ignores him, and then to everyone: his pleas mingle with the calls of the duelists. When he finds he can do nothing more and the authority of the Prince has no effect, he throws himself between the contestants. The stage direction, taken from the First Quarto, indicates that, in a mêlée, all is over suddenly and Tybalt hurries off.

thrust and move forward (dueling term)

fighting

runs him through

The fight between Tybalt and Mercutio has a mixture of daring and mockery. Zeffirelli's production in 1960 was high-spirited, like the words of the text: "Mercutio gaining possession of both swords, used one as a whetstone for the other before handing Tybalt's back—stopping to wipe its handle with mocking ostentation. With such preparation, Romeo could respond to Mercutio's sour jests after he is wounded as casually as the text demands—'Courage, man; the hurt cannot be much'—without appearing callow; the dying man's protestations could be taken as the holding up of an elaborate jest...The bragging turned to earnest all the more effectively with the suddenly involved and simple words of Romeo, 'I thought all for the best'" (*Shakespeare Survey* 15, 1962).

on dispatched

is not wounded

**86-97** In pain, Mercutio speaks with a new terseness. Only after the page has been sent to bring a

BENVOLIO What, art thou hurt?

MERCUTIO Ay, ay, a scratch, a scratch. Marry 'tis enough.
Where is my page? Go villain, fetch a surgeon. [*Exit* PAGE.]

ROMEO Courage, man; the hurt cannot be much.

MERCUTIO No, 'tis not so deep as a well, nor so wide as a church door; but 'tis enough,'twill serve. Ask for me tomorrow, and you shall find me a grave° man. I am peppered,° I warrant, for this world. A plague a' both your houses! Zounds,° a dog, a rat, a mouse, a cat, to scratch a man to death! A braggart, a rogue, a villain, that fights by the book of arithmetic!° Why the devil came you between us? I was hurt under your arm.

ROMEO I thought all for the best.

MERCUTIO Help me into some house Benvolio,
Or I shall faint. A plague a' both your houses!
They have made worms' meat of me.
I have it,° and soundly° too. Your houses!

*Exit* [*with* BENVOLIO.]

ROMEO This gentleman, the Prince's near ally,°
My very° friend, hath got this mortal hurt
In my behalf; my reputation stained
With Tybalt's slander—Tybalt, that an hour
Hath been my cousin. O sweet Juliet,
Thy beauty hath made me effeminate,
And in my temper° soft'ned valor's steel!

*Enter* BENVOLIO.

BENVOLIO O Romeo, Romeo, brave Mercutio is dead.
That gallant spirit hath aspired° the clouds,
Which too untimely here did scorn the earth.

ROMEO This day's black fate on moe days doth depend;°
This but begins the woe others must end.

[*Enter* TYBALT.]

BENVOLIO Here comes the furious Tybalt back again.

influential/buried    done for
by God's wounds
according to the rule book
I've been paid    fully
kinsman
true
character/quality (of steel)
risen to
threatens more days

doctor, does Romeo attempt to speak, using conventional expressions of cheer. At once Mercutio turns to him with savage and mordant wit, expressed in short, whipping phrases. When he has piled scorn on his adversary, he asks Romeo a terrible, direct question (ll. 96-7).

**98-102** Romeo's answer can help nobody, but he can say no more; Mercutio turns from him to Benvolio. To be rejected by his dying friend is a second terrible blow for Romeo; he remains silent, horrified and helpless, until after Mercutio has left the stage.

As Mercutio curses the rival houses for the third and fourth times (ll. 100, 102) and jests about the loss of all that was good in his own life, he will also be struggling to maintain consciousness: this is a last effort that wins close attention and, in almost every performance, admiration.

The deaths of Mercutio and Tybalt follow quickly on each other and make large demands on the actors. Together they give an impression of lacerating pain and huge psychological rifts and tensions; it seems, too, as if the strife has blazed into life from trivial causes, impelled by bad fortune.

**103-9** Romeo is left alone. (If other Montagues remain on-stage, they will stand at a distance; the Capulets have withdrawn with Tybalt.) He counts the cost and remembers Juliet. He is dazed, lost between the two realities of shame and love.

**110-14** Benvolio enters, visibly shaken by Mercutio's death. Romeo is silent at first; then he sees disaster closing in on him and in a clinching couplet voices his despair. He, too, is transformed: in II.vi.24-9, he had imagined endless joy; now he can see only an irreversible sequence of "woe."

**115-25** The sight of Tybalt "in triumph," surround-

ROMEO Alive in triumph, and Mercutio slain?
Away to heaven respective lenity,°
And fire-eyed° fury be my conduct° now!
Now Tybalt take the "villain" back again
That late thou gavest me; for Mercutio's soul
Is but a little way above our heads,
Staying for thine to keep him company.
Either thou or I, or both, must go with him.

TYBALT Thou wretched boy, that didst consort° him here,
Shalt with him hence.

ROMEO This° shall determine that.

[*They fight.* TYBALT *falls.*]

BENVOLIO Romeo away, be gone!
The citizens are up,° and Tybalt slain.
Stand not amazed. The Prince will doom thee death
If thou art taken. Hence, be gone, away!

ROMEO O I am fortune's fool!

BENVOLIO Why dost thou stay?

*Exit* ROMEO.

*Enter* CITIZENS.

CITIZENS Which way ran he that killed Mercutio?
Tybalt, that murderer, which way ran he?

BENVOLIO There lies that Tybalt.

CITIZEN Up sir, go with me.
I charge thee in the Prince's name obey.

*Enter* PRINCE, *old* MONTAGUE, CAPULET, *their* WIVES, *and all.*

PRINCE Where are the vile beginners of this fray?

BENVOLIO O noble Prince, I can discover° all
The unlucky manage° of this fatal brawl.
There lies the man, slain by young Romeo,
That slew thy kinsman, brave Mercutio.

LADY CAPULET Tybalt, my cousin! O my brother's child!

discriminating gentleness
i.e., from hell guide

ed by Capulets, inflames Romeo's shame; in a moment, he has committed himself to revenge. He goes to Tybalt, challenges him, and insists on a fight to death. Tybalt accepts Romeo's challenge with brief insults, and they fight "like lightning" (see line 165). The change in Romeo is huge: gone are responses "soft'ned" by love and the "fury" of revenge possesses him. No one dares interfere and Tybalt falls without a word. Romeo stands silent over the corpse.

accompany

i.e., his sword

in arms

Calling on "fire-eyed fury" (l. 118), Henry Irving "blazed" as Romeo: "There was not a nerve, not a muscle of him that did not quiver in passion...His eyes darted fire. His rapier was a whip. No hope for Tybalt; Romeo was past his guard in a flash" (We *Saw Him Act*, ed. H. A. Saintsbury et al., 1939, p. 226). At the Barbican, London, in 1987, Sean Bean's Romeo reacted more crudely, "in a sudden electrifying crescendo of energy, spreadeagling Tybalt...and stabbing him to a nasty death" (*Guardian*, 16 Apr.).

**126-39** By line 127, cries are heard offstage. Despite Benvolio's entreaties, Romeo remains stunned, silently appalled by what he has done until his rending, helpless cry of line 130. At Stratford-upon-Avon in 1958, Richard Johnson cried out "O, I am Fortune's fool!" in an "agonised shriek" that rang through the whole theater (*Scotsman* [Edinburgh], 4 Aug. 1958). Benvolio has to make him see the need for flight; in performance he often has to grapple with Romeo before the spell is broken. Without another word, Romeo runs off leaving Benvolio on the ground (see l. 133).

The stage fills quickly with a noisy crowd and Benvolio is arrested. Only the Prince's arrival brings an uneasy silence in which Benvolio does his best to explain in few words. Mention of his kinsman Mercutio, whose corpse is not on-stage, must directly affect the Prince.

reveal
handling

**140-44** Lady Capulet breaks through the ring of

O Prince! O cousin! Husband! O the blood is spilled
Of my dear kinsman. Prince, as thou art true,
For blood of ours shed blood of Montague.

PRINCE Benvolio, who began this bloody fray?

BENVOLIO Tybalt, here slain, whom Romeo's hand did slay.
Romeo, that spoke him fair, bid him bethink
How nice° the quarrel was, and urged withal°
Your high displeasure. All this, utterèd
With gentle breath, calm look, knees humbly bowed,
Could not take truce with the unruly spleen°
Of Tybalt deaf to peace, but that he tilts°
With piercing steel at bold Mercutio's breast;
Who, all as hot, turns deadly point to point,
And, with a martial scorn, with one hand beats
Cold death aside, and with the other sends
It back to Tybalt, whose dexterity
Retorts° it. Romeo he cries aloud,
"Hold friends! Friends, part!" and swifter than his tongue,
His agile arm beats down their fatal points,
And 'twixt them rushes; underneath whose arm
An envious° thrust from Tybalt hit the life
Of stout Mercutio, and then Tybalt fled;
But by and by° comes back to Romeo,
Who had but newly entertained° revenge,
And to 't they go like lightning; for ere I
Could draw to part them, was stout° Tybalt slain.
And as he fell, did Romeo turn and fly.
This is the truth, or let Benvolio die.

LADY CAPULET He is a kinsman to the Montague:
Affection° makes him false; he speaks not true.
Some twenty of them fought in this black strife,
And all those twenty could but kill one life.
I beg for justice, which thou, Prince, must give.
Romeo slew Tybalt; Romeo must not live.

PRINCE Romeo slew him; he slew Mercutio:
Who now the price of his dear blood doth owe?°

MONTAGUE Not Romeo, Prince; he was Mercutio's friend;
His fault concludes but what the law should end,

spectators with wild cries and a demand for revenge. In most productions, her words are taken up by other Capulets until the Prince again commands silence and attention for Benvolio.

**145-68** The accusation of Tybalt (l. 145) is likely to be greeted with vocal reactions from both sides, but especially by those who were present to see that Mercutio, in some ways, was the more provocative of the first two duelists. But Benvolio continues to give a careful detailed report, emphasizing all that is in Romeo's favor. He speaks as if he stood on trial for his own life (see l. 168). The regularity of the meter, with most sentences beginning in mid-line, suggests a steady, even-paced delivery despite Benvolio's difficulties and the violence that is described.

Line 167 is not strictly true, as the audience may recognize having just seen Romeo's delay. For the second time, Benvolio also minimizes Mercutio's role in inciting the fight. Having finished his account, he kneels before the Prince (l. 168). Attention then transfers to the Prince as Capulets and Montagues, now standing in two separate antagonistic groups, await judgment.

trivial besides

come to terms with ungovernable anger

thrusts

returns

full of enmity

immediately

engaged in

valiant, proud

partiality

who now is to pay the penalty for killing Mercutio

**169-90** Before the Prince can speak—his own sense of loss may inhibit him from taking command at once—Lady Capulet passionately asserts her sense of injustice and again begs for revenge. The Prince speaks carefully and with simple frankness. When Montague takes up his question, revealing his own partiality, the Prince proceeds to judgment, taking over in mid-line and so without hesitation (ll. 179-80). He publicly acknowledges his own sense of loss and uses this to impress both families with his determination to make them repent.

Rhyme accentuates the unanswerable authority of his speech, which silences all other response (see ll. 186-8). The sentence is heard in silence, and then

The life of Tybalt.

PRINCE And for that offense,
Immediately we do exile him hence.
I have an interest in your hate's proceeding:
My blood° for your rude brawls doth lie a-bleeding;
But I'll amerce° you with so strong a fine
That you shall all repent the loss of mine.
I will be deaf to pleading and excuses;
Nor tears nor prayers shall purchase out abuses;°
Therefore use none. Let Romeo hence in haste,
Else when he is found, that hour is his last.
Bear hence this body, and attend our will:
Mercy but murders, pardoning those that kill.°

*Exit [with others.]*

Scene ii *Enter* JULIET *alone.*

JULIET Gallop apace, you fiery-footed steeds,°
Towards Phoebus' lodging! Such a wagoner
As Phaëton° would whip you to the west,
And bring in cloudy night immediately.
Spread thy close° curtain, love-performing night,
That runaway's eyes° may wink,° and Romeo
Leap to these arms, untalked of and unseen.
Lovers can see to do their amorous rites,
By their own beauties; or if love be blind,
It best agrees with night. Come civil° night,
Thou sober-suited matron all in black,
And learn° me how to lose a winning match,°
Played for a pair of stainless maidenhoods.
Hood° my unmanned° blood, bating in my cheeks,
With thy black mantle, till strange° love grown bold,
Think true love acted simple modesty.
Come night; come Romeo;° come, thou day in night;
For thou wilt lie upon the wings of night
Whiter than new snow upon a raven's back.

the Prince leaves abruptly. He is followed by two slow processions, the Capulets bearing Tybalt's body: everyone is aware of loss and punishment to come. This new, extended silence, wholly different in kind from those before the fights, can be deeply affecting in performance, suggesting not only grief but also bewilderment at the swift turn of fortune.

(Mercutio is his kinsman)

punish

At Stratford, Ontario, in 1987, the nurse had entered among the crowd at l. 134: "after everyone had exited, she was left alone on the stage…[in] confusion and anxiety" (*Shakespeare Quarterly*, 39).

buy pardon for crimes

if mercy pardons murderers, it murders others by letting killers go free

Scene ii

horses of the sun god, Phoebus

son of Phoebus, killed for driving the sun chariot dangerously

secret

night's eyes (i.e., stars)

close

well-behaved

teach     surrender myself and gain a lover

blindfold     untrained (term of falconry) / unmated

shy

(wordplay on "knight")

**1-31** The use of successive imperatives and the wealth and variety of images combine to give an impression of eager impatience and rapture. The direct physical reference of several key verbs suggests that Juliet's performance should be active and alert: see "gallop…whip…spread" and, especially, "Leap to these arms," which implies that her arms are open as if to receive Romeo.

Lines 14-6 are probably very quiet. Immediately afterward, Juliet imagines Romeo to be with her, as in erotic daydream, with sensations of light, levitation, darkness, and virginal cold and whiteness. The next invocation speaks of death and a heavenly, nonhuman world, two repeated signifyers for dreams of sexual fulfillment in this tragedy. Juliet then returns to an awareness of her own impatience and helplessness (ll. 26-31). She no longer gazes into the night as at the beginning of the soliloquy but moves about restlessly or tries to sit and wait patiently. She responds at once to the first sound of the nurse's return.

Come gentle night, come loving, black-browed night,
Give me my Romeo; and when he shall die,
Take him and cut him out in little stars,
And he will make the face of heaven so fine
That all the world will be in love with night,
And pay no worship to the garish sun.
O I have bought the mansion of a love,
But not possessed it; and though I am sold,
Not yet enjoyed. So tedious is this day
As is the night before some festival
To an impatient child that hath new robes
And may not wear them. O here comes my nurse,

*Enter* NURSE, *with cords.*

And she brings news; and every tongue that speaks
But Romeo's name speaks heavenly eloquence.
Now Nurse, what news? What hast thou there, the cords°
That Romeo bid thee fetch?

NURSE Ay, ay, the cords.

JULIET Ay me, what news? Why dost thou wring thy hands?

NURSE Ah weraday!° He's dead, He's dead, He's dead!
We are undone lady, we are undone.
Alack the day! He's gone, he's killed, he's dead!

JULIET Can heaven be so envious?°

NURSE Romeo can,
Though heaven cannot. O Romeo, Romeo!
Who ever would have thought it? Romeo!

JULIET What devil art thou that dost torment me thus?
This torture should be roared in dismal° hell.
Hath Romeo slain himself? Say thou but "Ay,"
And that bare vowel "I" shall poison more
Than the death-darting eye of cockatrice.°
I am not I, if there be such an "Ay,"
Or those eyes'° shut that make thee answer "Ay."
If he be slain, say "Ay"; or if not, "No."
Brief sounds determine of° my weal or woe.

i.e., the rope ladder

**35** The nurse delays her response and then answers flatly. At once Juliet registers what the audience has seen on the nurse's entry—that she is broken with grief; she has also just recovered from a faint (see line 56). The contrast with the nurse's earlier manner, and with Juliet's preceding soliloquy, accentuates the effect of this entry.

alas

spiteful

**37-51** The nurse's repetitive and simple outcries at the beginning of her reply (ll. 37-42) suggest a stunned or distracted delivery. Juliet's first questioning response (l. 40) is in strong contrast and suggests that she moves or turns away from the nurse, as if lost, incredulous, or outraged. The repetition of Romeo's name, in loathing as well as disbelief, is more than Juliet can take without attacking the nurse in anger and demanding clearer knowledge. Then, as the nurse falls silent, Juliet in a flash faces a terrible impossibility (l. 45), and the sharp pangs of her feeling are expressed in fierce, self-punishing puns. At line 48, her whole world seems to dissolve, and she demands certain knowledge. Lines 50-1 show her trying to regain reasonable control and resolution.

dreadful, evil

basilisk (fabulous creature that killed with a look)

i.e., Romeo's (puns on *Ay, I*)

decide about/put an end to

In modern productions, many lines are cut from this duologue between the nurse and Juliet on the grounds of needless repetition and over elaborate rhetoric and imagery. But the writing is varied dramatically, so that each reaction is clearly realized.

NURSE I saw the wound, I saw it with mine eyes—
God save the mark!°—here on his manly breast.
A piteous corse,° a bloody piteous corse;
Pale, pale as ashes, all bedaubed in blood,
All in gore-blood. I swounded° at the sight.

JULIET O break, my heart! Poor bankrupt,° break at once!
To prison, eyes; ne'er look on liberty!
Vile earth,° to earth resign;° end motion here,
And thou and Romeo press one heavy° bier!

NURSE O Tybalt, Tybalt, the best friend I had!
O courteous Tybalt, honest gentleman,
That ever I should live to see thee dead!

JULIET What storm is this that blows so contrary?
Is Romeo slaught'red, and is Tybalt dead?
My dearest cousin, and my dearer lord?
Then, dreadful trumpet, sound the general doom,°
For who is living, if those two are gone?

NURSE Tybalt is gone, and Romeo banishèd;
Romeo that killed him, he is banishèd.

JULIET O God! Did Romeo's hand shed Tybalt's blood?

NURSE It did, it did! Alas the day, it did!

JULIET O serpent heart, hid with a flow'ring face!
Did ever dragon keep° so fair a cave?
Beautiful tyrant, fiend angelical,
Dove-feathered raven, wolvish-ravening lamb,
Despisèd° substance of divinest show—
Just° opposite to what thou justly seem'st—
A damnèd saint, an honourable villain!
O nature, what hadst thou to do in hell
When thou didst bower° the spirit of a fiend
In mortal paradise of such sweet flesh?
Was ever book containing such vile matter
So fairly bound? O that deceit should dwell
In such a gorgeous palace!

NURSE There's no trust,
No faith, no honesty in men; all perjured,

God help us

corpse

fainted

(pun: *break* = go bankrupt)

i.e., her body    commit yourself

weighty/mournful

doomsday, end of the world

live in/guard

despicable

exact

accommodate*

Shakespeare wrote for a boy actor who might have been better able to represent Juliet's feelings if her response to such shattering news is built up point by point. With clear vocal delivery and suitable variation of pitch and tempo, with regard for rhyme and meter, and with a physical response to both sound and meaning, the episode can have a musical and dance-like power; the complicated language is part of a virtuoso expression of emotional meaning.

**52-61** Still able to speak only in short phrases, the nurse gives the main facts as she saw them. Details of blood and deathly pallor come last at which Juliet breaks down, having held herself silent and, probably, quite still while the nurse was speaking.

At line 57, Juliet addresses only herself, not the nurse: she wills to die and becomes silent again only when she imagines herself to be with Romeo. After line 60 she is probably weeping, and the nurse with her.

**61-68** When the nurse regains her ability to speak, Juliet's attention is caught once more by Tybalt's name. After a moment's hesitation, she plunges into still more hopeless and savage despair: she faces the total destruction of her world and sees it like a final day of judgement.

**69-71** At first Juliet seems to catch her breath at what she hears. Then after an exclamation, she seeks confirmation with a terrible precision.

**73-85** The press of images suggests a reeling imagination and a mind struggling to encompass a multitude of nightmare sensations—bestial, garish, obscene, destructive, and, also, delicate, loving, pure, innocent. The speed and thrust of thought is suggested most vividly by line 78, in which the savage pun on *just* indicates a mind trying to catch up with sensations. For a moment, at lines 80-4, Juliet is able to question all her former moral judgements.

If the implication of each word in this speech is realized in performance, Juliet will seem passionate, pathetic, courageously clear-headed, and torn in many opposing directions.

**85-97** Juliet is quieted by the nurse's dismissal of all men and then the nurse is free to look around for Peter and feel pity for herself. When she curses

All forsworn, all naught,° all dissemblers.
Ah, where's my man? Give me some *aqua vitae.*°
These griefs, these woes, these sorrows make me old.
Shame come to Romeo!

JULIET Blistered be thy tongue
For such a wish! He was not born to shame:
Upon his brow shame is ashamed to sit;
For 'tis a throne where honor may be crowned
Sole monarch of the universal earth.
O what a beast was I to chide at him!

NURSE Will you speak well of him that killed your cousin?

JULIET Shall I speak ill of him that is my husband?
Ah, poor my lord, what tongue shall smooth thy name°
When I, thy three-hours wife, have mangled it?
But wherefore, villain, didst thou kill my cousin?
That villain cousin would have killed my husband.
Back, foolish tears, back to your native spring!
Your tributary drops° belong to woe,
Which you, mistaking, offer up to joy.°
My husband lives, that° Tybalt would have slain;
And Tybalt's dead, that would have slain my husband.
All this is comfort. Wherefore weep I then?
Some word there was, worser than Tybalt's death,
That murd'red me. I would forget it fain.°
But O, it presses to my memory,
Like damnèd guilty deeds to sinners' minds.
"Tybalt is dead, and Romeo banishèd."
That "banishèd," that one word "banishèd,"
Hath slain ten thousand Tybalts. Tybalt's death
Was woe enough, if it had ended there;
Or if sour woe delights in fellowship
And needly will be ranked with° other griefs,
Why followed not, when she said "Tybalt's dead,"
"Thy father" or "thy mother"—nay, or both—
Which modern° lamentation might have moved?°
But with a rearward,° following Tybalt's death,
"Romeo is banishèd!" To speak that word
Is father, mother, Tybalt, Romeo, Juliet,
All slain, all dead. "Romeo is banishèd":

wicked

spirits, brandy

Romeo, however, Juliet is jolted out of her silence: in a moment, she knows that her image of Romeo is wholly opposed to that of the nurse. She is angry and, then, she is wholly transformed, her words gaining authority as a regal image gathers strength in her mind. She "chides" herself and at line 97 answers the shocked comment of the nurse with simple dignity.

speak well of you*

**98-126** In the first of these lines, Juliet experiences pity for Romeo, self-reproach, and helpless wonder at the appalling event that has suddenly destroyed all her confidence and powers of action. Tears alternate with words and silence (see lines 102, 107, 109, 126), joy with grief: the switches of mood and the search for some adequate response and understanding can make this speech the most painful in the scene.

tears paying a tribute

i.e., she weeps for joy, because Romeo is alive

whom

At line 108, Juliet tries to understand by remembering the nurse's exact words and then, as all is recalled, repeating them (l. 112). Probably she breaks down again before working through the implications of "banished" and trying to understand all that it means. At line 124, she repeats "Romeo is banished" with flat hopelessness: violent reactions are spent, and she stares into the future that is now a blank for her, and then falls silent in despair.

willingly

For a moment, the nurse says, and probably does, nothing.

necessarily will be accompanied by

ordinary provoked

rear guard

There is no end, no limit, measure, bound,
In that word's death; no words can that woe sound.°
Where is my father and my mother, Nurse?

NURSE Weeping and wailing over Tybalt's corse.
Will you go to them? I will bring you thither.

JULIET Wash they his wounds with tears? Mine shall be spent,°
When theirs are dry, for Romeo's banishment.
Take up those cords. Poor ropes, you are beguiled—
Both you and I—for Romeo is exiled.
He made you for a highway to my bed;
But I, a maid,° die maiden-widowèd.
Come cords; come Nurse. I'll to my wedding bed;
And Death, not Romeo, take my maidenhead!

NURSE Hie to your chamber. I'll find Romeo
To comfort you. I wot° well where he is.
Hark ye, your Romeo will be here at night.
I'll to him; he is hid at Lawrence' cell.

JULIET O find him! Give this ring to my true knight
And bid him come, to take his last farewell.

*Exit* [*with* NURSE.]

Scene iii *Enter* FRIAR LAWRENCE.

FRIAR Romeo come forth; come forth, thou fearful° man.
Affliction is enamored of thy parts,
And thou art wedded to calamity.°

[*Enter* ROMEO.]

ROMEO Father, what news? What is the Prince's doom?
What sorrow craves acquaintance at my hand
That I yet know not?

FRIAR Too familiar
Is my dear son with such sour company.

utter / fathom (puns on *measure,* etc.)

**127-37** With a complete change of tone, Juliet asks the nurse a simple question. Behind it lies a sense of isolation (see lines 130-1) which will lead her to a decision to commit suicide (see lines 135-7). She gives a brief order to the nurse (l. 132) but then nearly breaks down as she remembers why the ropes have been brought. By the last couplet, however, she has recovered and calls the nurse to prepare for a solemn death.

expended

(pun on *made,* line 134)

**138-43** Realizing what is at stake, the nurse acts rapidly. "Hark ye" suggests that Juliet does not understand at first, or else has nearly fainted or collapsed into the nurse's arms. When Juliet does speak it is with instantaneous relief. With even greater speed of thought, she takes off a ring to give the nurse for Romeo. The two exits are abrupt: Juliet hurries to her room and the nurse, anxious to save life, follows as quickly as she can.

know

## Scene iii

full of fear / frightening

affliction is your lover and calamity your wife

**1-9** The friar arrives with news, but Romeo's entry is delayed so that the scene begins slowly. Romeo is deeply dejected and comes onstage like a man in chains or submissive to orders—in strong contrast to Juliet's preceding exit. He asks for news without hoping for relief. As Juliet had done (III.ii.67-8), Romeo sees the catastrophe as a "doomsday" (9), a judgement on the entire world. His ironic notion of "sorrow" politely introducing itself to his attention (see l. 5) is probably spoken with an anger that is under control only because it has spent its fury and now possesses him fully.

I bring thee tidings of the Prince's doom.

ROMEO What less than doomsday° is the Prince's doom?

FRIAR A gentler judgment vanished° from his lips:
Not body's death, but body's banishment.

ROMEO Ha, banishment? Be merciful, say "death";
For exile hath more terror in his look,
Much more than death. Do not say "banishment."

FRIAR Hence from Verona art thou banishèd.
Be patient, for the world is broad and wide.

ROMEO There is no world without° Verona walls,
But purgatory, torture, hell itself.
Hence banishèd is banished from the world,
And world's exile° is death. Then "banishèd"
Is death mis-termed. Calling death "banishèd",
Thou cut'st my head off with a golden axe,
And smilest upon the stroke that murders me.

FRIAR O deadly sin! O rude unthankfulness!
Thy fault our law calls death; but the kind Prince,
Taking thy part, hath rushed° aside the law,
And turned that black word "death" to "banishment."
This is dear° mercy, and thou seest it not.

ROMEO 'Tis torture, and not mercy. Heaven is here,
Where Juliet lives; and every cat and dog
And little mouse, every unworthy thing,
Live here in heaven and may look on her;
But Romeo may not. More validity,°
More honorable state, more courtship° lives
In carrion° flies than Romeo. They may seize
On the white wonder of dear Juliet's hand
And steal immortal blessing from her lips,
Who, even in pure and vestal° modesty,
Still° blush, as thinking their own kisses° sin.
But Romeo may not, he is banishèd.
Flies may do this, but I from this must fly;
They are freemen, but I am banishèd.
And sayest thou yet that exile is not death?
Hadst thou no poison mixed, no sharp-ground knife,

day of judgment (i.e., death)

issued

**11-23** "Banishment" again links this scene with the previous one (see III.ii.108-26), but Romeo responds with immediate horror. The friar says nothing at first to Romeo's wild entreaty (l. 12) and then quietly repeats the news and counsels patience (ll. 15-6).

Fastening on the word "world" as well as "banishment", Romeo's racing thoughts seem to torture him whichever way he rephrases his punishment: it is as if his mind were capable of nothing but torturing itself. Scorning the hope the friar offers, Romeo attacks him as a hypocrite. He probably turns away: there is now a gulf between them.

outside

exile from the world

**24-52** The friar, continuing to reason with his "pupil" (II.iii.82), argues that "mercy" is being offered. Romeo rejects this word at once: but it has prompted him to think again of Juliet and, with the simple "Heaven is here," he acknowledges the power of his faith in her. For a few moments, tender and adoring thoughts mingle with his anger and sense of senseless dispossession: the image of a "little mouse" looking at Juiet is both acutely sensitive and outrageously, almost crazily, far-fetched.

At line 40, savage despair again fills Romeo's mind, his thoughts sharpened now into rapid antitheses by an awareness of defilement and pain. His words rush out, gathering force, until he turns on the friar incredulously (l. 43) and then with scorn and violent reproach (ll. 48-51).

If the actor playing Romeo fits action to his words (as Hamlet advises the actors; Hamlet, III.ii), his long speech will call for many varied and demanding physical reactions within a short space. He struggles to keep charge of violent and tender feelings that battle within him but, if he speaks without great, headlong, and varied energy, he could seem to give way to self-pity and so repel an audience's sympathy; in some modern and political realist productions, this reaction is encouraged and then a number of lines are usually cut to prevent too great a loss of forward interest.

swept

precious

value

courtliness/wooing

flesh-eating

virgin

always i.e., when Juliet's two lips touch each other every time they are closed

No sudden mean° of death, though ne'er so mean,°
But "banishèd" to kill me? "Banishèd?"
O Friar, the damnèd use that word in hell;
Howling attends it! How hast thou the heart,
Being a divine, a ghostly° confessor,
A sin-absolver, and my friend professed,
To mangle me with that word "banishèd?"

FRIAR Thou fond° mad man, hear me a little speak.

ROMEO O thou wilt speak again of banishment.

FRIAR I'll give thee armor to keep off that word;
Adversity's sweet milk, philosophy,
To comfort thee, though thou art banishèd.

ROMEO Yet° "banishèd?" Hang up° philosophy!
Unless philosophy can make a Juliet,
Displant a town, reverse a prince's doom,
It helps not, it prevails not. Talk no more.

FRIAR O then I see that madmen have no ears.

ROMEO How should they, when that wise men have no eyes?°

FRIAR Let me dispute° with thee of thy estate.°

ROMEO Thou canst not speak of that thou dost not feel.
Wert thou as young as I, Juliet thy love,
An hour but married, Tybalt murderèd,
Doting like me, and like me banishèd,
Then mightst thou speak, then mightst thou tear thy hair,
And fall upon the ground, as I do now,
Taking the measure of an unmade grave.°

*Knock* [*at door.*]

FRIAR Arise, one knocks. Good Romeo hide thyself.

ROMEO Not I; unless the breath of heartsick groans
Mist-like infold me from the search of eyes. [*Knock.*]

FRIAR Hark, how they knock! Who's there?—Romeo arise;
Thou wilt be taken.—Stay awhile!—Stand up; [*Knock.*]
run to my study.—By and by!°—God's will, what simpleness° is
this?—I come, I come! Who knocks so hard? *Knock.*

instrument base

Probably the friar's silence and stillness at last reduce Romeo to silence too; not until line 52 does the friar speak again, this time with a touch of irony in his reproof.

spiritual

foolish

**53-70** The friar's attempts to reason with Romeo only sharpen his awareness that the priest lives in another world, especially with the short phrases of lines 57 and 60. Then in the one sustained phrase of line 64, Romeo makes a reproach that is unanswerable, and the friar is silent.

still give up/execute by hanging

At this point, however, Romeo may break down and fall on the ground in the helpless and suicidal rage he describes a few lines later (ll. 68-70). The friar stays close to him, so that when Romeo speaks again it is with a simple reiteration of what torments him and that probably leaves him speechless but visibly suffering with "heartsick groans" (l. 72).

cannot see what is obvious

If the fall is delayed until line 69, Romeo may appear self-consciously dramatic, indulging in grief; again, in some productions, the part is interpreted in this way.

discuss situation

i.e., in readiness for death

**71-78** The sudden knock alarms the friar and his philosophizing stops at once. Alternately, he remains in charge, whispers urgently to Romeo, calls to the unknown caller, and summons his own wits. The change to prose gives the actor freedom to emphasize whichever response seems most important for his interpretation of the role: panic, good sense, deep concern for Romeo, or self-protective prudence.

immediately foolishness

Romeo, however, does nothing, except to repudiate the friar's concern and give himself over to grief. Here he may again indulge in self-pity, but lines 72-3 can

Whence come you? What's your will?

NURSE [*Within.*] Let me come in, and you shall know my errand.
I come from Lady Juliet.

FRIAR Welcome, then.

*Enter* NURSE.

NURSE O holy Friar, O tell me, holy Friar,
Where is my lady's lord? Where's Romeo?

FRIAR There on the ground, with his own tears made drunk.

NURSE O he is even in my mistress' case,
Just in her case! O woeful sympathy,°
Piteous predicament! Even so lies she,
Blubb'ring and weeping, weeping and blubb'ring.
Stand up, stand up! Stand, and you be a man.
For Juliet's sake, for her sake, rise and stand!
Why should you fall into so deep an O?°

ROMEO [*Rises.*] Nurse!

NURSE Ah sir, ah sir! Death's the end of all.

ROMEO Speakest thou of Juliet? How is it with her?
Doth she not think me an old° murderer,
Now I have stained the childhood of our joy
With blood removed but little from° her own?
Where is she? And how doth she? And what says
My concealed lady° to our canceled° love?

NURSE O she says nothing sir, but weeps and weeps;
And now falls on her bed, and then starts up,
And Tybalt calls; and then on Romeo cries,
And then down falls again.

ROMEO As if that name,
Shot from the deadly level° of a gun,
Did murder her, as that name's cursèd hand
Murdered her kinsman. O tell me Friar, tell me,
In what vile part of this anatomy°
Doth my name lodge? Tell me, that I may sack°
The hateful mansion.

also express a purposeful choice of oblivion and a longing for protection. This is a crucial moment for the actor of Romeo: a chance to lose or gain the audience's sympathy and understanding.

**79-91** The nurse is too hurried to notice Romeo at first, as she runs to the friar for help. When she does see Romeo, she stands for a few lines wondering at his feelings and then, in Juliet's name, sharply rebukes him. When Romeo hears and responds, and struggles to his feet, her words almost stop (l. 91): now she can only exclaim in sympathy and express a conventional acceptance of death and suffering. Usually, she weeps unashamedly, so that Romeo has almost to support her.

agreement in suffering

a groan

hardened/aged

closely related to

secret wife annulled (by banishment)

**92-97** For a moment Romeo seems close to Juliet: at first he can speak of the terrible events and his own complicity with a new gentleness as he also remembers the "childhood" of their joy. When the nurse says nothing more, shorter phrases and a pun show that he again becomes urgent and keenly aware of his loss.

**98-117** The nurse's simple and repetitive phrases can be spoken dully, as if her feelings have been numbed by sorrow; or she can speak emphatically, still passionate with grief or determined that Romeo shall understand.

Romeo is quick to follow her thoughts in self-blame and nightmarish fantasy. Again he is ready for suicide and, with heavy and bitter irony, turns to ask the friar for wisdom as he "offers to stab himself" (this stage direction is from the First Quarto).

aim

As the friar forcibly remonstrates, the nurse disarms Romeo. In a moment, probably without a struggle, he is broken and weeping. He says nothing to the friar's reproaches now (compare lines 57-64).

body/corpse

pillage/destroy

[*He offers to stab himself, and* Nurse *snatches the dagger away.*]

Friar Hold thy desperate hand.
Art thou a man? Thy form cries out thou art;
Thy tears are womanish, thy wild acts denote
The unreasonable° fury of a beast.
Unseemly woman in a seeming man,
Or ill-beseeming beast in seeming both!°
Thou hast amazed me. By my holy order,
I thought thy disposition° better tempered.°
Hast thou slain Tybalt? Wilt thou slay thyself?
And slay thy lady, that in thy life lives,
By doing damnèd° hate upon thyself?
Why railest thou on thy birth, the heaven, and earth?
Since birth and heaven and earth, all three do meet
In thee at once; which thou at once wouldst lose.°
Fie, fie, thou shamest thy shape, thy love, thy wit,
Which° like a usurer° abound'st in all,
And usest none in that true use indeed
Which should bedeck thy shape, thy love, thy wit.
Thy noble shape is but a form of wax,°
Digressing° from the valor of a man;
Thy dear love sworn but hollow perjury,
Killing° that love which thou hast vowed to cherish;°
Thy wit, that ornament to shape and love,
Misshapen in the conduct° of them both,
Like powder° in a skilless soldier's flask,°
Is set afire by thine own ignorance,
And thou dismemb'red with thine own defense.°
What, rouse thee, man! Thy Juliet is alive,
For whose dear sake thou wast but lately dead:°
There° art thou happy.° Tybalt would kill thee,
But thou slewest Tybalt: there art thou happy.
The law, that threat'ned death, becomes thy friend
And turns it to exile: there art thou happy.
A pack of blessings light up upon thy back;
Happiness courts thee in her best array;
But like a misbehaved and sullen wench,
Thou pout'st upon thy fortune° and thy love.
Take heed, take heed, for such die miserable.
Go get thee to thy love, as was decreed;°

irrational

strange and unruly animal in acting like both man and woman

character ordered

(suicide is a mortal sin)

family, soul, and body unite in you, and you wish to destroy them at one stroke

who (puns on *use* = lend out at interest, and = copulate)

only a waxwork figure

in that it deviates

in that it kills (in marriage ceremony)

guidance

gunpowder container for gunpowder

blown to pieces by your own gunpowder

as good as dead in that respect (emphatic) fortunate

good fortune

arranged beforehand

**118-34** In modem productions, the friar's counsel is usually heavily cut. But his ordered argument allows him to reestablish his authority over Romeo and over the audience. The well-controlled similes and metaphors are violent and heroic, so that the friar is clearly trying to shock as well as reason. The catalogues at lines 121 and 124 suggest a pedagogic pointing of the lines, but "killing" and "set afire" express a contrary sense of alarm and passionate involvement. "Rouse thee" of line 134 suggests that by then Romeo has become entirely quiet and motionless.

**135-44** By repeating the simple words "happy" and "heed," the friar tries to get basic facts to register. Now he is close to Romeo, speaking more intimately and sympathetically; often he kneels by Romeo's side, supporting him in his arms.

**145-54** Romeo says nothing to the friar's plan, but

Ascend her chamber; hence and comfort her.
But look thou stay not till the watch be set,°
For then thou canst not pass to Mantua,
Where thou shalt live till we can find a time
To blaze° your marriage, reconcile your friends,
Beg pardon of the Prince, and call thee back
With twenty hundred thousand times more joy
Than thou went'st forth in lamentation.
Go before, Nurse. Commend me to thy lady,
And bid her hasten all the house to bed,
Which heavy sorrow makes them apt unto.
Romeo is coming.

NURSE O Lord, I could have stay'd here all the night
To hear good counsel. O what learning is!
My lord, I'll tell my lady you will come.

ROMEO Do so, and bid my sweet prepare to chide.°

[NURSE *offers to go in and turns again.*]

NURSE Here sir, a ring she bid me give you sir.
Hie you, make haste, for it grows very late. [*Exit.*]

ROMEO How well my comfort° is revived by this!

FRIAR Go hence; good night. And here stands all your state:°
Either be gone before the watch be set,
Or by the break of day disguised from hence.
Sojourn in Mantua. I'll find out your man,
And he shall signify° from time to time
Every good hap to you that chances here.
Give me thy hand. 'Tis late. Farewell; good night.

ROMEO But that a joy past joy calls out on me,
It were a grief, so brief° to part with thee.
Farewell. *Exeunt.*

guard is posted (at the city gates)

make known publicly

scold

delight

on this depends all your fortune

give news

hurriedly

he must give some sign of assent and of returning hope that encourages his advisor.

Even when the friar concludes with the expectation of a peaceful life with Juliet, Romeo is still silent; renewed hope must be working on his imagination, bringing life back to body and mind, but in such a way that it cannot yet be expressed in words. It is a recovery from near death made in silence. With so much at stake in the narrative, Romeo's smallest reactions to the friar's words will register clearly with the audience.

The friar shows that he expects Romeo's cooperation by turning to instruct the nurse in what to do in consquence (l. 154).

**157-60** At line 157, the friar speaks for Romeo who is now standing in acquiescence. The incomplete verse-line suggests a pause as the nurse realizes how completely Romeo has changed. Her amazed and facile praise of learning can so break the tension that it raises a laugh.

**161-74** After a silence of more than fifty lines, Romeo speaks with a gentleness that also suggests a deep distrust of his own actions (161). All three figures onstage are silent as the nurse turns to go and then stops (as indicated in the First Quarto's stage direction) and another silence follows as Romeo takes the ring and the nurse leaves. Then Romeo turns to the friar and speaks for the first time of his renewed hope.

When the friar has given more instructions and explanations of his plans, he takes Romeo's hand in trust (l. 171). Only now does Romeo dare to use such a word as "joy;" this is enough, with very few more words, to move the action of the drama forward once more, impelled by Romeo's deepest and almost inexpressible feelings.

Scene iv *Enter old* CAPULET, LADY CAPULET, *and* PARIS.

CAPULET Things have fall'n out sir, so unluckily
That we have had no time to move° our daughter.
Look you, she loved her kinsman Tybalt dearly,
And so did I. Well, we were born to die.
'Tis very late; she'll not come down tonight.
I promise° you, but for your company,
I would have been abed an hour ago.

PARIS These times of woe afford no time to woo.
Madam, good night; commend me to your daughter.

LADY CAPULET I will, and know her mind early tomorrow;
Tonight she's mewed up° to her heaviness,°

CAPULET Sir Paris, I will make a desperate tender°
Of my child's love. I think she will be ruled
In all respects by me; nay more, I doubt it not.
Wife, go you to her ere you go to bed;
Acquaint her here of my son Paris' love
And bid her—mark you me?—on Wednesday next—
But soft, what day is this?

PARIS Monday, my lord.

CAPULET Monday! Ha, ha! Well, Wednesday is too soon;
A'° Thursday let it be. A' Thursday, tell her,
She shall be married to this noble earl.°
Will you be ready? Do you like this haste?
We'll keep no great ado—a friend or two—
For hark you, Tybalt being slain so late,
It may be thought we held him carelessly,°
Being our kinsman, if we revel much.
Therefore we'll have some half a dozen friends,
And there an end. But what say you to Thursday?

PARIS My lord, I would that Thursday were tomorrow.

## Scene iv

discuss the matter with

assure

shut up (as a young hawk when changing plumage) grief

bold offer

on

nobleman

did not pay him proper respect

**1-11** The tone is confidential, apologetic, and somewhat weary: the Capulets are bidding their noble guest farewell and he is being polite and discreet; a number of servants may be attending Paris and so emphasise his high ranking in Verona. For the audience, all this will seem very down-beat after the passionate intensity of the two lovers; however it also brings a sense of everyday affairs and unstressed behaviour that will re-establish the setting for the play's action. The contrast between this and the two preceding scenes marks the gulf between Juliet and her parents, and the inevitability of clashes to come. The three main figures on stage may even seem luckless, a small family group standing alone and unaware of the oncoming avalanche.

**12-36** At the last moment, Capulet makes an unexpected move. He addresses Paris and his wife individually and only pauses for a response when he needs to know the day or remembers that he still needs Paris's assent (ll. 18, 28). As he busily assumes command of the situation, the audience will realize that he is precipitating a catastrophe.

Ironically, the tone and rhythms of the scene can be lightened still further in performance so that Capulet becomes a figure of comedy, a secure fool in his own house. Such an effect would be accentuated by reactions from the others onstage or it could be inhibited by Lady Capulet expressing criticism or suspicion by making a point of her silence and lack of enthusiasm.

Line 29 is important for the actor playing Paris, an opportunity for showing either a conventional politeness or a sincere admiration of Juliet.

However the episode is played, Capulet's concluding jest brings laughter on himself. The scene ends on a small upbeat as the servants, who have been called at line 33, hurry to precede their master with torches or lanterns.

CAPULET Well get you gone. A' Thursday be it then.
Go you to Juliet ere you go to bed;
Prepare her, wife, against° this wedding day.
Farewell, my lord.—Light to my chamber, ho!
Afore me,° it is so very late
That we may call it early by and by.°
Good night. *Exeunt.*

Scene v *Enter* ROMEO *and* JULIET, *aloft.*

JULIET Wilt thou be gone? It is not yet near day:
It was the nightingale, and not the lark,
That pierced the fearful° hollow of thine ear.
Nightly she sings on yond pomegranate tree.
Believe me love, it was the nightingale.

ROMEO It was the lark, the herald of the morn,
No nightingale. Look love, what envious streaks
Do lace° the severing clouds in yonder East.
Night's candles° are burnt out, and jocund day
Stands tiptoe on the misty mountaintops.
I must be gone° and live, or stay° and die.

JULIET Yond light is not daylight; I know it, I.
It is some meteor° that the sun exhales
To be to thee this night a torchbearer,
And light thee on thy way to Mantua.
Therefore stay yet; thou need'st not to be gone.

ROMEO Let me be ta'en, let me be put to death;
I am content, so thou wilt have it so.
I'll say yon gray is not the morning's eye,°
'Tis but the pale reflex° of Cynthia's° brow;
Nor that is not the lark whose notes do beat
The vaulty heaven so high above our heads.
I have more care° to stay than will° to go.
Come death, and welcome! Juliet wills it so.
How is't, my soul? Let's talk; it is not day.

in expectation of

indeed (a light oath)
soon

fearing

mark with gold*
stars

(pun: *gone* = die) (pun: *stay*=be secure, remain alive)

(the sun was supposed to draw up vapors and ignite them as meteors; they were ill omens)

sun at first peep of day
reflection the moon's

concern/wish desire/willingness

Scene v

**1-23** The stage is usually empty for a little while between scenes; sometimes birdsong is heard. Then Romeo comes silently onto the balcony and, after another pause, Juliet follows him. With such preparation, the audience will attend closely to the quiet talk and respond to both its urgency and suggestions. Rhythm, description, and imagery all show the lovers to be held still in a shared sense of wonder that is more powerful than their spoken fears. References to the sun, night, mountains, meteors, and the "vaulty heaven" suggest both the immensity of their sensations and the inevitable changes of fate in which thoughts of "death" are close to those of life.

In modem productions, this scene is often played on a bed, as if in Juliet's bedroom; in this case, the setting has to be complicated or the text altered because Romeo must say lines 58-9 as if outside the house and at a lower level (see l. 55). In Elizabethan performances, lines 1-68 were probably played from the balcony, with Romeo climbing down and leaving across the main stage; Lady Capulet would then enter on the main stage at line 65, and Juliet, having left the balcony after line 67, would reappear below at line 69.

Productions in nineteen-nineties, especially those using translated texts, have staged this scene so that sexual contact between the lovers is intimate and sustained; the differences between them can become brash and comedic. Karin Beier's Dusseldorf production is an example: "You'd think they'd just been through some cheap one-night stand, judging by the tetchy morning-after, complete with slaps on the face and a sort of did-didn't slanging match over whether they can hear a nightingale or a lark" (*Independent*, 2 Nov. 1994).

**24-40** As Romeo makes a joke about his own death (l. 24), Juliet is silent. He goes on to pretend

JULIET It is, it is! Hie° hence, be gone, away!
It is the lark that sings so out of tune,
Straining harsh discords and unpleasing sharps.°
Some say the lark makes sweet division;°
This doth not so, for she divideth us.
Some say the lark and loathèd toad change° eyes;
O now I would they had changed voices too,
Since arm from arm° that voice doth us affray,°
Hunting thee hence with hunt's-up° to the day.
O now be gone! More light and light it grows.

ROMEO More light and light: more dark and dark our woes.

*Enter* NURSE.

NURSE Madam!

JULIET Nurse?

NURSE Your lady mother is coming to your chamber.
The day is broke; be wary, look about. [*Exit.*]

JULIET Then window let day in, and let life° out.

ROMEO Farewell, farewell! One kiss, and I'll descend.
[*He goes down.*]

JULIET Art thou gone so, love? Lord? Ay, husband! friend!°
I must hear from thee every day in the hour,
For in a minute there are many days.°
O by this count° I shall be much in years°
Ere I again behold my Romeo!

ROMEO Farewell!
I will omit no opportunity
That may convey my greetings, love, to thee.

JULIET O think'st thou we shall ever meet again?

ROMEO I doubt it not; and all these woes shall serve
For sweet discourses° in our times° to come.

JULIET O God, I have an ill-divining° soul!
Methinks I see thee, now thou art so low,
As one dead in the bottom of a tomb.

haste

shrill notes

rapid runs of music/separation

exchange

from each other's arms fright-en away

early morning hunting song

that they have time enough for any "talk." This alerts Juliet and she becomes urgently and wholly concerned for his safety and tries to continue the earlier argument, bending it to her newly felt sense of danger. With the cruel image of a hunt, she gives up all other arguments to persuade Romeo to "be gone." Romeo realizes that they cannot claim the "light" any more and for a moment the two lovers come together in bitter awareness that they stand against the whole course of the world and its power. They probably embrace until roused by the nurse's entry and alarm.

i.e., Romeo

**41-42** Few words now accompany rapid actions, but they are highly charged with feeling. After one more kiss, with determined speed, Romeo climbs down from the balcony.

lover

because time (without Romeo) seems endless

reckoning much older

**43-63** Once Romeo is safely away from the house, Juliet calls after him in a whisper. With line 43, she seems to realize all she has enjoyed and lost; and then she looks towards the future. For a moment, now that danger of discovery is not so immediate, they both speak simply, as if holding back their feelings or being too spent to express tumultuous sensations.

pleasant talks life

foreseeing evil

**54-59** Leaning over the balcony, Juliet shudders with a new fear and then cries out: as she gazes into her husband's face, her worst fear for the future seems realized in the present. As if they were,

Either my eyesight fails, or thou lookest pale.

ROMEO And trust me, love, in my eye° so do you;
Dry° sorrow drinks our blood.° Adieu, adieu! *Exit.*

JULIET O Fortune, Fortune, all men call thee fickle!
If thou art fickle, what dost thou with him
That is renowned for faith? Be fickle, Fortune;
For then I hope thou wilt not keep him long,
But send him back.

*Enter* LADY CAPULET.

LADY CAPULET Ho daughter, are you up?

JULIET Who is't that calls? It is my lady mother.
Is she not down so late,° or up so early?
What unaccustomed° cause procures° her hither?

LADY CAPULET Why how now, Juliet?

JULIET Madam I am not well.

LADY CAPULET Evermore weeping for your cousin's death?
What, wilt thou wash him from his grave with tears?
And if thou couldst, thou couldst not make him live;
Therefore have done. Some grief shows much of love;
But much of grief shows still° some want of wit.

JULIET Yet let me weep, for such a feeling° loss.

LADY CAPULET So shall you feel the loss, but not° the friend
Which you weep for.

JULIET Feeling so the loss,
I cannot choose but ever weep the friend.°

LADY CAPULET Well girl, thou weep'st not so much for his death
As that the villain lives which slaughtered him.

JULIET What villain madam?

LADY CAPULET That same villain Romeo.

JULIET [*Aside.*] Villain and he be many miles asunder.—
God pardon him! I do, with all my heart;
And yet no man like he° doth grieve my heart.

view
thirsty (so taking color from the cheeks)

already, almost lifeless—sorrow having drained all blood from their bodies—they part with hardly another word. Juliet cannot say farewell; line 70 suggests that she is on the point of tears, perhaps weeping already.

**60-69** Alone, Juliet cries out against her fate and her mind races to comprehend what has happened. Her mother's call brings Juliet back to immediate concerns and, speaking to herself, she rapidly tries to understand what is happening. When she confronts her mother (for the staging, see note, lines 1-23), she takes time before answering, as indicated by the metrical irregularity. She probably struggles to overcome tears.

so late getting to bed
strange brings

**70-105** At first Juliet takes her mother's words in her own very different sense, and so is able to speak freely of Romeo (l. 78). At line 81, however, this is no longer possible and, after a brief aside, she begins a series of puns that allows her passion some outlet in words. Although her instinctive subterfuge almost breaks down at line 95—Juliet shudders with horror and yearning, as the syntax buckles and breaks under the strain—she continues carefully and tensely, keeping her feelings as subdued as possible.

always

deep felt

but not be affected by

Lines 97-103 are strangely quiet, full-hearted, and cruel, so that Lady Capulet believes that the talk of revenge, with all its savagery, has pacified her daughter. After the briskly reassuring, yet murderous, line 104, Lady Capulet changes the subject; usually she accompanies her words with a bright smile.

lover

The degree of intimacy appropriate for this scene is not easily gauged. At line 70, some Lady Capulets sit by Juliet's side (on her bed if this is now onstage) and take her in their arms; if so played, Juliet must break away at line 81 so that her next speech may be spoken aside. Other Lady Capulets show that they want to embrace Juliet here or on line 79, or, with added irony, on line 85, but are prevented by Juliet's reserve or her movement away. Others stand throughout, either cold or as if determined to

as he does (by his absence)

LADY CAPULET That is because the traitor murderer lives.

JULIET Ay madam, from the reach of these my hands;°
Would none but I might venge my cousin's death!°

LADY CAPULET We will have vengeance for it, fear thou not.
Then weep no more. I'll send to one in Mantua,
Where that same banished runagate° doth live,
Shall give him such an unaccustomed dram°
That he shall soon keep Tybalt company;
And then I hope thou wilt be satisfied.°

JULIET Indeed I never shall be satisfied.°
With Romeo till I behold him . . . Dead . . .
Is my poor heart so for a kinsman vexed.°
Madam, if you could find out but a man
To bear a poison, I would temper° it;
That Romeo should, upon receipt thereof,
Soon sleep in quiet.° O how my heart abhors
To hear him named and cannot come to him,
To wreak° the love I bore my cousin
Upon his body that° slaughtered him!

LADY CAPULET Find thou the means, and I'll find such a man.
But now I'll tell thee joyful tidings, girl.

JULIET And joy comes well in such a needy time.
What are they, beseech your ladyship?

LADY CAPULET Well, well, thou hast a careful father, child;
One who, to put thee from thy heaviness,°
Hath sorted out° a sudden day of joy
That thou expects not, nor I looked not for.

JULIET Madam, in happy time!° What day is that?

LADY CAPULET Marry, my child, early next Thursday morn,
The gallant, young and noble gentleman,
The County° Paris, at Saint Peter's Church,
Shall happily make thee there a joyful bride.

JULIET Now by Saint Peter's Church and Peter too,
He shall not make me there a joyful bride!
I wonder at this haste, that I must wed
Ere he that should be husband comes to woo.

take command; this makes a strong contrast with Juliet's fugitive helplessness and search for some kind of strength.

(for lovemaking/for vengeance)
(so Romeo would be spared/so vengeance might be fit)

In the modern dress production at the Shakespeare Theatre, Washington, D.C., in 1994, Lady Capulet "held a wine glass and was slightly drunk" throughout this scene, as if "deeply unhappy over Tybalt's death and trying to dull the pain" (*Shakespeare Quarterly*, 46).

fugitive
unlooked for dose (of poison)

repaid

sexually fulfilled

distressed

mix/modify

die/sleep peacefully

avenge/express
the body of him who

**106-16** Spent with tears and the acute suffering brought on by her mother's inquiries, Juliet gathers courage and speaks at first with a simplicity that conceals deep irony. Lady Capulet seems to hold back her news (ll. 114-6) until she thinks she is sure of Juliet's attention.

sorrow
arranged

Most, but not all, Lady Capulets sit by their daughter here and take her hands, kissing or embracing her—see the more intimate "child" at lines 108 and 113. The concluding "joyful bride" invites more intimacy but, instead, it may well release more tears or nervous laughter.

it's the right time

Count

**117-26** Juliet's response is instantaneous and strong, and sharpened by an ironic echo of her mother's words. Julia Marlowe, as Juliet, spoke the two lines with "a full, sweeping implication...of that reserve power that was to carry her to the threshold

I pray you tell my lord and father, madam,
I will not marry yet; and when I do, I swear
It shall be Romeo, whom you know I hate,
Rather than Paris. These are news indeed!

LADY CAPULET Here comes your father. Tell him so yourself,
And see how he will take it at your hands.

*Enter* CAPULET *and* NURSE.

CAPULET When the sun sets the air doth drizzle dew:
But for the sunset of my brother's son°
It rains downright.
How now? A conduit,° girl? What, still in tears?
Evermore show'ring? In one little body
Thou counterfeits° a bark, a sea, a wind:
For still° thy eyes, which I may call the sea,
Do ebb and flow with tears; the bark thy body is,
Sailing in this salt flood;° the winds, thy sighs,
Who, raging with thy tears and they with them,
Without a sudden calm° will overset
Thy tempest-tossèd body. How now wife?
Have you delivered to her our° decree?

LADY CAPULET Ay sir; but she will none,° she gives you thanks.
I would the fool were married to her grave!

CAPULET Soft, take me with you,° take me with you, wife.
How? Will she none? Doth she not give us thanks?
Is she not proud?° Doth she not count her blest,
Unworthy as she is, that we have wrought°
So worthy a gentleman to be her bride?°

JULIET Not proud° you have, but thankful, that you have.
Proud can I never be of what I hate,
But thankful even for hate that is meant° love.

CAPULET How, how, how, how, chopped-logic?° What is this?
"Proud," and "I thank you," and "I thank you not":
And yet "not proud"? Mistress minion° you,
Thank me no thankings, nor proud me no prouds,
But fettle° your fine joints 'gainst Thursday next
To go with Paris to Saint Peter's Church,

of suicide rather than renounce her love...The next instant she has reminded herself that she must play a part," and addresses her mother with studied politeness (C. E. Russell, *Julia Marlowe* [[1926], p.] 235).

Juliet contrives to speak covertly of Romeo and their marriage until, after the effort of the sudden assertion, she falls silent or breaks into tears again on "These are news indeed."

As Capulet is heard from offstage—he may knock at the door, or swear at the nurse who is trying to prevent his entry—Lady Capulet turns away without offering Juliet the slightest comfort.

(pun on *sun*)

water fountain, spout

resembles

constantly

sea (poetic)

unless there is an unexpected calm

my (royal plural; pompous)

will have none of it

**127-42** Capulet is confident that his plan for Juliet's marriage to Paris will solve everything, so he teases Juliet about her tears, with heavy and self-conscious humour considering them as rain and a storm at sea. Perhaps the half-line 129 indicates a pause in which Capulet tries to make contact with his daughter and she turns away from him. He seems oblivious of anything wrong until his wife, with harsh brevity, answers him.

wait, speak so that I can understand

pleased

arranged

bridegroom

sexually excited (?)

intended for

cheap argument

hussy

make ready

**142-58** Capulet changes tone at once, looking incredulously and accusingly at Juliet. All eyes will be on her as she answers carefully. Her last line (149) seems a bid for loving understanding, which she had not attempted with her mother. Capulet fails to respond, becoming more enraged, mocking, and, at line 156, threatening.

As Juliet remains pale and silent, he abuses her so violently that his wife again intervenes (l. 158).

Or I will drag thee on a hurdle thither.°
Out you green-sickness carrion!° Out you baggage,
You tallow-face!°

LADY CAPULET Fie, fie! What, are you mad?

JULIET Good father, I beseech you on my knees,
Hear me with patience but to speak a word.

CAPULET Hang thee, young baggage! Disobedient wretch!
I tell thee what: get thee to church a° Thursday,
Or never after look me in the face.
Speak not, reply not, do not answer me!
My fingers itch.° Wife, we scarce thought us blest
That God had lent us° but° this only child,
But now I see this one is one too much,
And that we have a curse in having her.
Out on her, hilding!°

NURSE God in heaven bless her!
You are to blame my lord, to rate° her so.

CAPULET And why, my Lady Wisdom? Hold your tongue,
Good prudence. Smatter with your gossips,° go!

NURSE I speak no treason.

CAPULET O, God-i-god'en!°

NURSE May not one speak?

CAPULET Peace, you mumbling fool!
Utter your gravity o'er a gossip's bowl,
For here we need it not.

LADY CAPULET You are too hot.

CAPULET God's bread,° it makes me mad!
Day, night, hour, tide, time, work, play,
Alone, in company:—still° my care hath been
To have her matched; and having now provided
A gentleman of noble parentage,
O fair demesnes,° youthful, and nobly trained,°
Stuffed,° as they say, with honorable parts,°
Proportioned as one's thought would wish a man—
And then to have a wretched puling° fool,

(as traitors went to execution)
anemic piece of dead flesh
pale-faced creature

on

i.e., to box her ears
given into our keeping
only

jade, trollop

scold

save your prattle for your cronies

God give you good evening (impatiently)

by the sacred host

continually

domains educated
furnished/full qualities

whimpering

**159-98** Juliet now moves quickly and, with simple earnestness, falls on her knees before her father, begging him to listen. At this, his frustration reaches its climax, so that his "fingers itch" (l. 165); since immediately afterwards he is rather less powerfully assertive, his whole body may be shaking, as if he were about to have a stroke.

The nurse's intervention only aggravates his fury, turning it momentarily on her at lines 171-72. His wife's second intervention makes him swear and leads to a self-justification that betrays the helplessness of his passion. Mocking Juliet again (ll. 187-8), he makes his threats with repetitive emphasis. At lines 191-4, he adds still greater threats and strives to become terribly solemn. Juliet says nothing, and everyone else is silent. Again he threatens and, at line 195, he makes an oath on his immortal salvation to disown his daughter. He seems wholly carried away with the assertion of his will and, with three more very short warnings, he leaves the stage without a word to his wife and without waiting for any response from Juliet.

Capulet's angry speeches are brutal to the defenseless Juliet, but in some performances his inability to listen to anyone and the disproportionate violence of his language give an effect that is partly comic or pathetic, or, even, pathological. At Stratford, Ontario, in 1992, on "Look to't, think on't, I do not use to jest" [Capulet] suddenly took her in his arms and delivered his ultimatum quietly and coldly. At the conclusion of his speech, he embraced her tightly and kissed her full on the lips to the obvious consternation of Lady Capulet, who looked awary, and the Nurse, who gazed at them deeply troubled" (*Shakespeare Quarterly*, 46).

A whining mammet,° in her fortune's tender,°
To answer "I'll not wed, I cannot love;
I am too young, I pray you pardon me!"
But, an° you will not wed, I'll pardon you!°
Graze° where you will, you shall not house with me.
Look to't, think on't; I do not use to jest.°
Thursday is near; lay hand on heart,° advise.°
An° you be mine, I'll give you to my friend;
An you be not, hang, beg, starve, die in the streets,
For by my soul, I'll ne'er acknowledge thee,
Nor what is mine shall never do thee good.
Trust to't. Bethink you. I'll not be forsworn. *Exit.*

JULIET Is there no pity sitting in the clouds
That sees into the bottom of my grief?
O sweet my mother, cast me not away!
Delay this marriage for a month, a week;
Or if you do not, make the bridal bed
In that dim monument where Tybalt lies.

LADY CAPULET Talk not to me, for I'll not speak a word.
Do as thou wilt, for I have done with thee. *Exit.*

JULIET O God! O Nurse, how shall this be prevented?
My husband is on earth, my faith° in heaven;
How shall that faith return again to earth,°
Unless that husband send it me from heaven,
By leaving earth?° Comfort me, counsel me.
Alack, alack, that heaven should practice stratagems°
Upon so soft° a subject as myself!
What say'st thou? Hast thou not a word of joy?
Some comfort, Nurse.

NURSE Faith, here it is.
Romeo is banished; and all the world to nothing
That he dares ne'er come back to challenge you;°
Or if he do, it needs must be by stealth.
Then since the case so stands as now it doth,
I think it best you married with the county.
O, he's a lovely gentleman!
Romeo's a dishclout to him. An eagle, madam,
Hath not so green, so quick, so fair an eye

puppet when she is offered a good chance of marriage

if give you leave to go (pun)

feed

am not in the habit of joking

consider the truth take thought

if

**198-206** Capulet's exit is followed by an incredulous silence, which Juliet is the first to break with the quiet voice of despair. She then turns to her mother, now calling her "sweet"; the new earnestness, however, soon reverts to despair. As Lady Capulet briefly rejects her daughter and leaves, Juliet exclaims "O God!" and then turns to her only other helper, the nurse. The two usually come together seeking mutual comfort.

marriage vow

how shall I be freed from my vow

i.e., by dying

contrive traps/devise violent attacks

tender hearted/yielding

**207-14** The nurse is silent at first, but in most productions she takes Juliet in her arms at once. Juliet now speaks more freely, without having to hide her love for Romeo, and yet she envisions only her husband's death and sees fate as perverse. She is more helpless than ever, acknowledging the need of "comfort": after her brave assertions and her silences, she can seem like a child again.

there's not a hope in the world that he will ever dare return to claim you

**215-27** Juliet will listen eagerly at first, but this cannot last. As the nurse voices her proposal, the half-line 220 suggests a pause in which the audience may see Juliet catch her breath before the nurse proceeds with facile praise of Paris.

As Paris hath. Beshrew° my very heart,
I think you are happy in this second match,
For it excels your first; or if it did not,
Your first is dead, or 'twere as good he were,
As living here and you no use of him.

JULIET Speak'st thou from thy heart?

NURSE And from my soul too; else beshrew them both.

JULIET Amen!

NURSE What?

JULIET Well, thou hast comforted me marvelous much.
Go in, and tell my lady I am gone,
Having displeased my father, to Lawrence' cell,
To make confession and to be absolved.

NURSE Marry, I will; and this is wisely done. [*Exit.*]

JULIET Ancient damnation!° O most wicked fiend!
Is it more sin to wish me thus forsworn,°
Or to dispraise my lord with that same tongue
Which she hath praised him with above compare°
So many thousand times? Go, counselor!
Thou and my bosom° henceforth shall be twain.°
I'll to the Friar to know his remedy.
If all else fail, myself have power to die. *Exit.*

cursed be

**228-36** Juliet's solemn question is dramatically opposed to the nurse's growing confidence in the comfort she is offering. The silences, indicated by the break down of the iambic verse at lines 228-31 are ominous: Juliet's "Amen" will be fervent and, with the simple "What?", the nurse seems to suspect something is wrong. Much is at stake but, as Juliet continues and covers up her true response, the nurse is reassured and leaves quickly.

damned old woman/ancient devil

false to marriage vows

as being beyond comparison

secret thoughts

separated

**237-44** Juliet's condemnation of the nurse marks the moment when she knows she is totally without help, betrayed by the woman who had always supplied affection and flattery. Usually in performance there is a moment of stillness and silence before the words of line 237 ring out. Juliet seems to gather strength from them: now she knows that she must stand alone and that she has more strength than her companion and confidante. After her dismissal of past affection and trust (ll. 241-2), her exit is accompanied by only a few words: their effect is to heighten the audience's expectation and suspence; for the actress they are an opportunity to express either a new confidence, courage, panic, or cold determination—whatever she judges a fitting close to the violent scene—as Juliet's inner feelings are at last freely expressed and she finds that she is unafraid to die.

# ACT IV

Scene i *Enter* FRIAR LAWRENCE *and* COUNTY PARIS.

FRIAR On Thursday sir? The time is very short.

PARIS My father Capulet will have it so,
And I am nothing slow to slack his haste.°

FRIAR You say you do not know the lady's mind.
Uneven° is the course; I like it not.

PARIS Immoderately she weeps for Tybalt's death,
And therefore have I little talked of love;
For Venus smiles not in a house of tears.
Now sir, her father counts it dangerous
That she doth give her sorrow so much sway,
And in his wisdom hastes our marriage
To stop the inundation of her tears,
Which, too much minded by herself alone,°
May be put from her° by society.°
Now do you know the reason of this haste.

FRIAR [*Aside.*] I would I knew not why it should be slowed.—
Look sir, here comes the lady toward my cell.

*Enter* JULIET.

PARIS Happily met, my lady and my wife!

JULIET That may be sir, when I may be a wife.°

PARIS That "may be" must be, love, on Thursday next.

JULIET What must be shall be.

FRIAR That's a certain text.°

ACT IV. Scene i

**1-16** The friar's short phrases and his aside at line 16 show him to be agitated and, unusually, at a loss to give advice and counsel. He may walk nervously to and fro as he listens and deliberates. In contrast, Paris speaks fluently, as if he knows all that is to be said about this socially acceptable and arranged marriage. Line 15, repeating the "Now" from line 9, can be said after a pause in which he has waited for the friar's approval; or it can be said so that it indicates an underlying impatience.

no reluctance on my part will lessen his haste

irregular

brooded on in her solitude

from her mind

companionship

**17-38** As the friar hesitates, he sees Juliet but does not greet her, unless silently with the sign of the cross as she kneels before him. Paris takes the initiative and the speeches of one or two lines that follow, in which each speaker takes words carefully from the other, represent a wary encounter. Juliet's half-line (21) is probably an attempt to terminate the talk, with the friar seconding her with his one interjection. Paris, however, changes the subject and presses his attentions on Juliet again; he continues to do so despite her longer speeches. By line 29, he is probably standing very close to her; she will look down or turn away.

Until line 26, Paris may well sound callow and overpersistent, but a slow tempo for this duologue, or

after I am married/when I am free to marry

true saying

PARIS Come you to make confession to this father?

JULIET To answer that, I should confess° to you.

PARIS Do not deny to him that you love me.

JULIET I will confess to you that I love him.

PARIS So will ye, I am sure, that you love me.

JULIET If I do so, it will be of more price,°
Being spoke behind your back, than to your face.

PARIS Poor soul, thy face is much abused° with tears.

JULIET The tears have got small victory by that,
For it was bad enough before their spite.°

PARIS Thou wrong'st it more than tears with that report.

JULIET That is no slander sir, which is a truth;
And what I spake, I spake it to my face.°

PARIS Thy face is mine, and thou hast sland'red it.

JULIET It may be so,° for it is not mine own.°
Are you at leisure holy father now,
Or shall I come to you at evening mass?

FRIAR My leisure serves me, pensive daughter now.
My lord, we must entreat the time alone.°

PARIS God shield° I should disturb devotion!
Juliet, on Thursday early will I rouse ye.
Till then adieu, and keep this holy kiss. *Exit.*

JULIET O shut the door, and when thou hast done so,
Come weep with me: past hope, past care, past help!

FRIAR O Juliet, I already know thy grief;
It strains° me past the compass° of my wits.
I hear thou must, and nothing may prorogue° it,
On Thursday next be married to this county.°

JULIET Tell me not, friar, that thou hearest of this,
Unless thou tell me how I may prevent it.
If in thy wisdom thou canst give no help,
Do thou but call my resolution wise

make my confession / admit my feelings

a few pauses, will communicate to the audience underlying uncertainties on both sides. Juliet's conscious effort is to keep up appearances, and her inner tension becomes almost unbearable before she turns to the friar at line 37.

value

spoiled

hostile action

openly / about my face

i.e., slandered (it belongs to Romeo)

ask to have this time to ourselves

forbid

**39-45** The friar extricates Juliet at once by asking Paris to leave. Juliet says nothing, even submitting to Paris's parting kiss at line 43, and only when he is safely gone does she entreat the friar's sympathy. Line 45 suggests that she breaks down in tears as the friar hurries to shut the door.

taxes limits

can postpone

Count

**46-67** After the friar has closed the door, much depends on how the two meet: he may go at once to comfort Juliet or he can stand still, uncertain how to act; or she can run sobbing to him.

When the friar gives no counsel or comfort, but only repeats what they both know, Juliet's earnest passion breaks out impatiently. Three times she says she will kill herself (ll. 54, 59, 62-5). The first time she is urgent, surprizing him (and the audience) by showing that she has a knife ready for the act. The second time she again shows the knife but is more solemn and implicates the friar in her decision. The last time,

And with this knife I'll help it presently.°
God joined my heart and Romeo's, thou our hands;
And ere this hand, by thee to Romeo's sealed,
Shall be the label° to another deed,°
Or my true heart with treacherous revolt
Turn to another, this shall slay them both.°
Therefore out of thy long-experienced time,°
Give me some present counsel; or behold,
'Twixt my extremes° and me this bloody° knife
Shall play the umpire, arbitrating that
Which the commission° of thy years and art
Could to no issue of true honor bring.
Be not so long to speak: I long to die
If what thou speak'st speak not of remedy.

FRIAR Hold daughter, I do spy a kind of hope,
Which craves as desperate an execution
As that is desperate which we would prevent.
If rather than to marry County Paris,
Thou hast the strength of will to slay thyself,
Then is it likely thou wilt undertake
A thing like death to chide° away this shame,°
That° cop'st° with death himself to scape from it;
And if thou darest, I'll give thee remedy.

JULIET O bid me leap, rather than marry Paris,
From off the battlements of any tower,
Or walk in thievish ways,° or bid me lurk
Where serpents are; chain me with roaring bears,
Or hide me nightly in a charnel house,°
O'ercovered quite with dead men's rattling bones,
With reeky° shanks and yellow chapless° skulls;
Or bid me go into a new-made grave
And hide me with a dead man in his shroud—
Things that, to hear them told, have made me tremble—
And I will do it without fear or doubt,
To live an unstained wife to my sweet love.

FRIAR Hold then: go home, be merry, give consent
To marry Paris. Wednesday is tomorrow:
Tomorrow night look that thou lie alone,
Let not thy nurse lie with thee in thy chamber.

immediately

bear the seal act/legal document

i.e., *hand* and *heart*

lifetime

extremities, sufferings cruel

authority (continuing legal terminology)

scold, drive disgrace

you who encounters/matches

roads frequented by thieves

mortuary

dank, rank smelling jawless

the friar having made no response, she says very little but, with a bitter pun on "long" (l. 66), ensures that her deliberate resolve is unmistakable and that she has a positive appetite for certainty and consummation.

**68-76** The friar's first words seek to restrain Juliet; he may do so physically as well, perhaps touching her for the first time. As soon as he speaks, however reservedly, of "hope," Juliet's attention is caught. She quickly becomes still and intent, and he continues carefully and quietly.

**77-89** As Juliet quickly offers to undertake the friar's instructions, the imagery suggests how thoughts of danger and death lead her to imagine a nightmarish horror which mixes sexual contact and physical corruption. The parenthetical line 86 shows that she is able to recognize how wholly new and surprising her state of mind is: it also helps to emphasize the control with which she speaks the simple and touching affirmation with which she concludes. Tears and violent reactions are over as she prepares to listen to the friar. His first words of brief instruction show that he accepts her resolution absolutely, without question.

**89-117** Although the friar's instructions go contrary to all her instincts, Juliet is now silent and attentive. The friar speaks with quiet voice and even tempo, being careful to let her know exactly what to do and what will happen. He watches her intently, testing her

Take thou this vial, being then in bed,
And this distilling° liquor drink thou off;
When presently through all thy veins shall run
A cold and drowsy humor.° For no pulse
Shall keep his native° progress, but surcease;°
No warmth, no breath, shall testify thou livest.
The roses in thy lips and cheeks shall fade
To wanny° ashes, thy eyes' windows° fall
Like death when he shuts up the day of life.
Each part, deprived of supple government,°
Shall, stiff and stark and cold, appear like death;
And in this borrowed likeness of shrunk death
Thou shalt continue two-and-forty hours,
And then awake as from a pleasant sleep.
Now, when the bridegroom in the morning comes
To rouse thee from thy bed, there art thou dead.
Then as the manner of our country is,
In thy best robes uncovered° on the bier
Thou shalt be borne to that same ancient vault
Where all the kindred of the Capulets lie.
In the meantime, against° thou shalt awake,
Shall Romeo by my letters know our drift,°
And hither shall he come; and he and I
Will watch thy waking, and that very night
Shall Romeo bear thee hence to Mantua.
And this shall free thee from this present shame,
If no inconstant toy° nor womanish fear
Abate thy valor in the acting it.°

JULIET Give me, give me! O tell not me of fear!

FRIAR Hold; get you gone. Be strong and prosperous°
In this resolve. I'll send a friar with speed
To Mantua, with my letters to thy lord.

JULIET Love give me strength, and strength shall help afford.°
Farewell dear father. *Exit* [*with* FRIAR.]

penetrating

fluid

natural stop

pale, wan eyelids

ability to control movement of the limbs

with face uncovered

by the time that

purpose, plot

sudden dislike

carrying it out

successful

provide

resolution by her reactions.

By giving the friar this kind of exposition after the urgency of Juliet's pleas and the hesitancy of his first reactions, Shakespeare has ensured that the audience is fully and soberly acquainted with the most extraordinary and implausible elements of his story: the audience's attention, like the friar's, will be fixed on Juliet's response and as she believes what she is told, so will the audience.

**118-26** When the friar concludes by warning Juliet that all depends on her courage, her reply is simple and eager. She is transformed, possessed by a new hope and conscious of a new assurance in the power of "Love" (l. 125). Like the preceding four scenes, this one also ends quickly so that the audience's expectation is drawn forward strongly.

Juliet usually kisses the friar at line 126, before running offstage ahead of him; the half verse-line may indicate a momentary hesitation that would mark a continuing sense of risk. Sometimes the friar holds Juliet back for a moment as he silently blesses her.

Scene ii *Enter* CAPULET, LADY CAPULET, NURSE, *and two or three* SERVINGMEN.

CAPULET So many guests invite as here are writ.
[*Exit a* SERVINGMAN.]
Sirrah, go hire me twenty cunning° cooks.

SERVINGMAN You shall have none ill° sir; for I'll try if they can lick their fingers.°

CAPULET How canst thou try them so?

SERVINGMAN Marry sir, 'tis an ill cook that cannot lick his own fingers;° therefore he that cannot lick his fingers goes not with me.

CAPULET Go, begone. [*Exit* SERVINGMAN.]
We shall be much unfurnished° for this time.
What, is my daughter gone to Friar Lawrence?

NURSE Ay forsooth.

CAPULET Well, he may chance to do some good on her.
A peevish self-willed harlotry it is.

*Enter* Juliet.

NURSE See where she comes from shrift° with merry look.

CAPULET How now, my headstrong, where have you been gadding?

JULIET Where I have learnt me to repent the sin
Of disobedient opposition
To you and your behests, and am enjoined
By holy Lawrence to fall prostrate here
To beg your pardon. Pardon, I beseech you.
Henceforward I am ever ruled by you.

CAPULET Send for the county.° Go tell him of this.

skillful

no bad ones

relish food (lick their lips)

test their own food

unprepared

confession

Count

## Scene ii

**1-14** The busy coming-and-going is a relief from the tensions of IV.i; it also develops the audience's sense of expectation.

In contrast with Capulet's expansive mood (see line 2), his terse dismissal of the joking servant hints at an underlying unease. This becomes more explicit immediately before Juliet's entry.

**15-22** As the nurse directs attention to her, Juliet stands silent. "Merry" of line 15 suggests that she looks entirely different, but the nurse probably exaggerates: Juliet crosses the stage to kneel before her father with words that are solemn and deliberate in submission.

**23-32** Capulet responds energetically, trying to take control of the new situation in a series of short

I'll have this knot° knit up tomorrow morning.

JULIET I met the youthful lord at Lawrence' cell
And gave him what becomèd° love I might,
Not stepping o'er the bounds of modesty.

CAPULET Why, I am glad on't. This is well. Stand up.
This is as't should be. Let me see the county.
Ay marry, go, I say, and fetch him hither.
Now, afore God, this reverend holy friar,
Our whole city is much bound° to him.

JULIET Nurse, will you go with me into my closet,°
To help me sort° such needful ornaments
As you think fit to furnish° me tomorrow?

LADY CAPULET No, not till Thursday. There is time enough.

CAPULET Go Nurse, go with her. We'll to church tomorrow.
*Exeunt* [JULIET *and* NURSE.]

LADY CAPULET We shall be short in our provision;
'Tis now near night.

CAPULET Tush, I will stir about,
And all things shall be well, I warrant thee, wife.
Go thou to Juliet, help to deck up her.
I'll not to bed tonight; let me alone.°
I'll play the housewife for this once. What ho!
They are all forth.° Well, I will walk myself
To County Paris, to prepare up° him
Against° tomorrow. My heart is wondrous light,
Since this same wayward girl is so reclaimed.
*Exit* [*with* LADY CAPULET.]

Scene iii *Enter* JULIET *and* NURSE.

JULIET Ay, those attires are best. But gentle Nurse,
I pray thee leave me to myself tonight;
For I have need of many orisons°

marriage

as was fitting

phrases that express his pleasure, repeat his orders, tell Juliet what to do, and compliment the friar. The insecurity caused by the row with his daughter, that had threatened all his plans for her and for himself, can be seen in this behaviour; alternatively, it can be played as the habitual bullying of an overbearing nobleman and father. Either way, Capulet hardly speaks to Juliet who continues to kneel until after line 28.

indebted

private room

choose

attire

**33-35** With amazing calmness, Juliet acts her new part by taking the initiative to leave her father.

**36-47** The end of this scene has several cross-currents to Capulet's sudden happiness: twice his wife tries unsuccessfully to restrain him and, when he calls for servants (l. 43), he realizes that he has to do his errand himself.

Capulet leaves by a different exit than his wife. A moment's pause by Lady Capulet before she leaves can lightly underline Capulet's disproportionate haste and bouyant humor; it would also give the actress opportunity to express more fully, by bearing or gesture, the independent reactions implied by lines 36 and 38-9.

leave it to me

gone out

fully prepare

in time for

Scene iii

prayers

**1-13** The location has moved to Juliet's bedroom. The nurse, believing that her charge has accepted her advice (see III.v.232-6), brings clothes out of a closet; although silent, she is both officious

To move the heavens to smile upon my state,°
Which well thou knowest is cross° and full of sin.

*Enter* LADY CAPULET.

LADY CAPULET What, are you busy, ho? Need you my help?

JULIET No madam; we have culled such necessaries°
As are behoveful° for our state° tomorrow.
So please you, let me now be left alone,
And let the nurse this night sit up with you;
For I am sure you have your hands full all,
In this so sudden business.

LADY CAPULET Good night.
Get thee to bed, and rest; for thou hast need.
*Exeunt* [LADY CAPULET *and* NURSE.]

JULIET Farewell! God knows when we shall meet again.
I have a faint° cold fear thrills through my veins,
That almost freezes up the heat of life.
I'll call them back again to comfort me.
Nurse! What should she do here?
My dismal° scene I needs must act alone.
Come, vial.
What if this mixture do not work at all?
Shall I be married then tomorrow morning?
No, no! This shall forbid it. Lie thou there.
[*Lays down a dagger.*]
What if it be a poison, which the friar
Subtly° hath minist'red° to have me dead,
Lest in this marriage he should be dishonored
Because he married me before to Romeo?
I fear it is; and yet methinks it should not,
For he hath still been tried° a holy man.
How if, when I am laid into the tomb,
I wake before the time that Romeo
Come to redeem° me? There's a fearful point!°
Shall I not then be stifled in the vault,
To whose foul mouth no healthsome air breathes in,
And there die strangled° ere my Romeo comes?
Or if I live, is it not very like°

condition of being (spiritual)
wrong, perverse

i.e., wedding attire / the potion
necessary (archaic [?])
pomp

and watchful.

Juliet stands by the bed in which she had slept with her bridegroom the night before. She speaks carefully, with a pretense of confidence in the nurse. When her mother enters, she is no less polite but still firmer in requesting both to leave. Lady Capulet's brief response (ll. 12-3) can show some affection for her daughter or a guarded recognition that her child's manner is, in some strange way, alarming; or she can be wholly insensitive to Juliet, making only a conventional allusion to marriage pleasures. The nurse usually joins in with a laugh or a kiss before the two women leave as if without another thought.

causing faintness

fatal / cheerless

**14-29** Left alone, Juliet seems at first to be in command of herself, but after line 14 her whole body senses the terror of facing death and isolation. Impulsively she cries out "Nurse," usually running to the door. She stops abruptly, recognizing the inevitability of her fate and her own responsibility for action. The incomplete verse-lines 18 and 20 probably indicate tense silences. Resolute and, possibly, overly dramatic actions at lines 20 and 23 alternate now with thoughts of fear and insecurity.

treacherously provided

always been found to be

regain / save conclusion

suffocated
likely

**30-59** As soon as Juliet is prepared to trust the friar, she thinks of the moment of waking in the tomb. In her imagination, she suffers its stifling air. As she forces herself to think further of what will happen, her imagination feeds on images of death (ll. 36 ff.). The precise idea of Tybalt's dead body awakens fantasies of the spirits of the dead, terror, and madness. As her thoughts rush on, rhythms become wilder and images more physical and grotesque.

Many Juliets stand still, trembling, clutching, and shuddering; at lines 44-45, they become terribly quiet and still. Other Juliets run across the stage in several directions, as if seeking some escape. By line 48, most begin to be increasingly distracted or even childishly or lewdly and overtly mad; at line 54,

The horrible conceit° of death and night,
Together with the terror of the place—
As in a vault, an ancient receptacle,
Where for these many hundred years the bones
Of all my buried ancestors are packed;
Where bloody Tybalt, yet but green in earth,°
Lies fest'ring in his shroud; where, as they say,
At some° hours in the night spirits resort.
Alack, alack, is it not like that I
So early waking—what with loathsome smells,
And shrieks like mandrakes° torn out of the earth,
That° living mortals, hearing them run mad.
O if I wake, shall I not be distraught,°
Environèd with all these hideous fears,
And madly play with my forefathers' joints,
And pluck the mangled Tybalt from his shroud,
And in this rage,° with some great kinsman's bone,
As with a club, dash out my desp'rate brains?
O look! Methinks I see my cousin's ghost
Seeking out Romeo, that did spit his body
Upon a rapier's point. Stay, Tybalt, stay!
Romeo! Romeo! Romeo!
Here's drink. I drink to thee.

[*She falls upon her bed within the curtains.*]

Scene iv *Enter* Lady Capulet *and* Nurse [*with herbs.*]

Lady Capulet Hold, take these keys and fetch more spices, Nurse.

Nurse They call for dates and quinces in the pastry.

*Enter old* Capulet.

Capulet Come, stir, stir, stir! The second cock hath crowed,
The curfew bell hath rung, 'tis three o'clock.
Look to the baked meats,° good Angelica;°

perception, knowledge

freshly buried

certain

plant with forked root (supposed to grow under gallows and shriek when pulled up)

so that

sent out of my mind

madness

some seem about to mutilate themselves.

Then, suddenly at line 55, Juliet is transfixed, shocked, and stunned, as if actually seeing Tybalt with sword in hand. With "stay," Juliet reaches quickly for the vial and removes its stopper. She then takes total command of herself and pledges her love to Romeo: so she forgets her terror and the world she is about to leave. She drinks, waits perhaps for several moments, and then falls lifeless onto the bed.

In performance, Juliet's soliloquy can seem melodramatic, operatic, or overstrained and in the nineteenth century it very effectively ran that risk. A. C. Sprague's*Shakespeare and the Actors* (1944, pp. 310-4) notes many different interpretations: Mary Anderson's Juliet rushed to the door, stopped, and then drew the curtains across the window, paused and, "with her hand on the curtain, half wrapping it round her," stared back in silence at the vacant chamber; when she saw Tybalt's ghost, Adelaide Neilson's Juliet "swung round...with hands screening her eyes, as if recoiling from the sight, which yet fascinated her, of Tybalt's imagined shape behind her;" Madame Modjeska threw herself into a great chair and "with convulsive hands" beat off the "spectres of her imagination until love, stronger than terror, made her leap into their midst and shield Romeo."

At the end, every actress must choose how she affirms her love using the simplest words and the act of drinking to Romeo. After the tense and violent scene, such a concise action will gain the audience's closest attention.

If the varying feelings are expressed with truth and clarity and the expressive rhythms and language are respected, Juliet's last sustained solo scene will have overwhelming effect.

## Scene iv

**1-23** The location shifts again. In an Elizabethan theatre, the bed would remain on stage with its curtain drawn, ready for the following scene.

This brief scene of domestic business and bustle in preparation for the arrival of Paris is in great contrast with the previous one. Moreover, Shakespeare has made Capulet more like an English householder than a powerful head of a family in Renaissance Verona, perhaps with the intention of giving extra familiarity and credibility to the strange tale of fate and magic potions.

meat pies (the nurse's name)

The stage business is diversified by Capulet's

Spare not for cost.

NURSE Go, you cotquean,° go;
Get you to bed! Faith you'll be sick tomorrow
For this night's watching.°

CAPULET No, not a whit. What, I have watched ere now
All night for lesser cause, and ne'er been sick.

LADY CAPULET Ay, you have been a mouse-hunt° in your time;
But I will watch you from° such watching now.
*Exit* LADY CAPULET *and* NURSE.

CAPULET A jealous hood,° a jealous hood!

*Enter three or four* SERVINGMEN *with spits and logs and baskets.*

Now, fellow,
What is there?

FIRST SERVINGMAN Things for the cook sir; but I know not what.

CAPULET Make haste, make haste. [*Exit* FIRST SERVINGMAN.]
Sirrah, fetch drier logs.
Call Peter; he will show thee where they are.

SECOND SERVINGMAN I have a head sir, that will find out logs°
And never trouble Peter for the matter.

CAPULET Mass,° and well said! A merry whoreson,° ha!
Thou shalt be loggerhead.°
[*Exit* SECOND SERVINGMAN, *with Others.*]
Good faith, 'tis day.
The county will be here with music straight,°
For so he said he would. I hear him near. *Play music.*
Nurse! Wife! What ho! What, Nurse I say!

*Enter* NURSE.

Go waken Juliet; go and trim her up.
I'll go and chat with Paris. Hie,° make haste,
Make haste! The bridegroom he is come already.
Make haste I say. [*Exeunt.*]

insistence on speed and the continued criticism of him by both the nurse and Lady Capulet. Twice, Capulet is left onstage by himself (at lines 13 and 21-4), so that he will be seen to hold the center among all the busy running to and fro. His soliloquies show him to be anxious and boastful, rather than deeply concerned.

"old woman"

wakefulness

hunter of mice/women*

keep an eye on you to prevent

female, head

(because his head is wooden)

By the Mass bastard (jocular)

blockhead

immediately

**23-28** The bridal music played offstage, as if at a distance, gives an impression of the pressure of events and also a measured, graceful counterpoint to Capulet's urgent fuss.

In Elizabethan performances there would be no need for the nurse to leave the stage between this scene and the next; she would move back to open the curtains at the rear of the stage and so lead into the new scene by revealing Juliet's bed.

hurry

Scene v [*Enter* NURSE.]

NURSE Mistress! What, mistress! Juliet! Fast,° I warrant her, she.
Why lamb! Why lady! Fie, you slug-a-bed.
Why love, I say! Madam! Sweetheart! Why bride!
What, not a word? You take your pennyworths° now;
Sleep for a week, for the next night, I warrant,
The County Paris hath set up his rest,°
That you shall rest but little. God forgive me!°
Marry, and amen. How sound is she asleep.
I needs must wake her. Madam, madam, madam!
Ay, let the county take you in your bed;
He'll fright you up, i' faith. Will it not be?
[*Draws back the curtains.*]
What, dressed and in your clothes, and down° again?
I must needs wake you. Lady! Lady! Lady!
Alas, alas! Help, help! My lady's dead!
O weraday° that ever I was born!
Some *aqua vitae*° ho! My lord! My lady!

*Enter* LADY CAPULET.

LADY CAPULET What noise is here?

NURSE O lamentable day!

LADY CAPULET What is the matter?

NURSE Look, look! O heavy° day!

LADY CAPULET O me, O me! My child, my only life!
Revive, look up, or I will die with thee!
Help, help! Call help.

*Enter* CAPULET.

CAPULET For shame, bring Juliet forth; her lord is come.

## Scene v

fast asleep

**1-16** The location is, again, Juliet's bedroom. As she speaks to Juliet and to herself, the nurse is arranging clothes, jewels, and the various requirements of Juliet's toilet. She laughs at her own affectionate and bawdy jokes. At line 13, she touches Juliet, and by the end of the line she has become thoroughly alarmed. She calls out loudly in growing panic.

as much as you can afford

staked his all (with bawdy pun)

i.e., for speaking bawdily

A grotesque comedy can arise from the nurse's repeated cries and the rapid shifts of her attention in the first moments of alarm; but her cries must also betray such helplessness and panic that the simple repetitions become charged with emotional force. When Edith Evans played the nurse, her lamentations had "a queer high-pitched intensity" that compelled the audience to share her woe (*Manchester Guardian*, 14 March 1936).

gone to bed

alas

brandy

**17-21** Lady Capulet's questioning concern contrasts with the nurse's helpless words as she kneels by Juliet's bedside. At line 19, Lady Capulet takes in what has happened and then she too is stricken with grief, her words suggesting an entirely new intensity of feeling. The short line 21 may indicate that no one speaks for some time before Capulet's entry; perhaps both women are weeping.

sorrowful, black

The music accompanying Paris may still audible, gradually coming nearer to the bedroom.

NURSE She's dead. Deceased. She's dead, alack the day!

LADY CAPULET Alack the day, she's dead, she's dead, she's dead!

CAPULET Ha! Let me see her. Out alas she's cold,
Her blood is settled,° and her joints are stiff;
Life and these lips have long been separated.
Death lies on her like an untimely° frost
Upon the sweetest flower of all the field.

NURSE O lamentable day!

LADY CAPULET O woeful time!

CAPULET Death, that hath ta'en her hence to make me wail,
Ties up my tongue and will not let me speak.

*Enter* FRIAR LAWRENCE *and the* COUNTY PARIS, *with* MUSICIANS.

FRIAR Come, is the bride ready to go to church?

CAPULET Ready to go, but never to return.
O son, the night before thy wedding day
Hath Death lain with thy wife. There she lies,
Flower as she was, deflowered by him.
Death is my son-in-law, Death is my heir;
My daughter he hath wedded. I will die
And leave him all: life, living,° all, is Death's.

PARIS Have I thought long° to see this morning's face,
And doth it give me such a sight as this?

LADY CAPULET Accursed, unhappy, wretched, hateful day!
Most miserable hour that e'er time saw
In lasting labor° of his pilgrimage!
But one, poor one, one poor and loving child,
But one thing to rejoice and solace in,
And cruel death hath catched° it from my sight.

NURSE O woe! O woeful, woeful, woeful day!
Most lamentable day, most woeful day
That ever, ever, I did yet behold!
O day! O day! O day! O hateful day!

**23-32** The repetitions of the women are affectingly simple and eliminate almost all difference between the two characters. But they are confined within regular iambic pentameters and so do not hold up the action or weaken the forward pressure of the scene.

congealed

out of season

As Capulet sees and touches Juliet (see l. 25), he comments practically, as if forcing himself to realize all that has happened. Then the delicate and sustained image of lines 28-9 makes a surprising contrast, suggesting a sensitivity to his daughter that has not been so evident in earlier scenes. The women immediately cry out again and with some dignity Capulet also gives in to tears.

**33-40** The music bursts into full volume as the musicians accompany the groom and friar onto the stage. After Capulet's ironic and severe announcement, there will be a shocked silence, all the more impressive for the celebratory entry that precedes it. Capulet continues to speak with care, point, and self-lacerating wordplay; the others are silent, perhaps crossing themselves and going to kneel at the bedside. The musicians will stand at the door to the stage.

possessions

longed for

**41-64** The repetitive expressions of grief, the wordplay, apostrophes and antitheses, together with a sustaining and often insistent metrical regularity, give this scene a distinctive style. It can sound affected, self-conscious, or even, false in performance and this would be accentuated if the audience is made aware that the speakers' own losses, rather than Juliet's suffering, occupy their thoughts. Shakespeare may have chosen the explicit and artificial style in order to prevent grief for a counterfeit death from gaining too much of the audience's interest and sympathy; or, perhaps, in order to show the inadequacies of the speakers' feelings.

unceasing toil

snatched

The text is usually much cut in performance. Sometimes it is spoken with no attempt at realism of behaviour but with such musical tone of voice and carefully controlled variation that it is in a new way

Never was seen so black a day as this:
O woeful day! O woeful day!

PARIS Beguiled, divorcèd,° wrongèd, spited, slain!
Most detestable Death, by thee beguiled,
By cruel, cruel thee quite overthrown.
O love! O life! . . . not life, but love in death!

CAPULET Despised, distressèd, hated, martyred, killed!
Uncomfortable° time, why cam'st thou now
To murder, murder our solemnity?°
O child! O child! My soul, and not my child!
Dead art thou: alack, my child is dead,
And with my child my joys are burièd!

FRIAR Peace ho, for shame! Confusion's° cure lives not
In these confusions.° Heaven and yourself
Had part in this fair maid: now heaven hath all,
And all the better is it for the maid.
Your part in her° you could not keep from death,
But heaven keeps his part° in eternal life.
The most you sought was her promotion,
For 'twas your heaven° she should be advanced;°
And weep ye now, seeing she is advanced°
Above the clouds, as high as heaven itself?
O in this love, you love your child so ill
That you run mad, seeing that she is well.°
She's not well married that lives married long,
But she's best married that dies married young.°
Dry up your tears, and stick your rosemary°
On this fair corse and, as the custom is,
In all her best array bear her to church;
For though fond nature° bids us all lament,
Yet nature's tears are reason's merriment.°

CAPULET All things that we ordainèd° festival
Turn from their office° to black funeral:
Our instruments° to melancholy bells;
Our wedding cheer° to a sad burial feast;
Our solemn° hymns to sullen° dirges change;
Our bridal flowers serve for a buried corse;
And all things change them° to the contrary.

parted

cheerless

spoil the festivity

disaster's

commotions

her mortal body, begotten by you

her soul

idea of bliss honored

carried up

blessed in heaven (conventional phrase to use of the dead)

(because she knows no sorrow)

(for remembrance; used at funerals and weddings)

foolish human nature

seem foolish to right thinking

designed for

proper function

musical instruments

food/mirth

festival mournful

themselves

affecting. Lines 65-6, 73, and 76 suggest, however, that Shakespeare expected a spirited performance that would accentuate the violence of the words, the clashes of thought and feeling, and the weeping: played in this way, each character would strive to express individual feeling and yet each sound much alike as they "run mad" (76).

Some directors have had all four persons speak and cry out simultaneously, each in their own way and timing; this produces the impression of a general confusion and panic.

In the first Quarto, that probably reflects Elizabethan stage usage, the text of this scene is much shortened and replaced by a stage-direction: "All at once cry out and wring their hands."

**65-84** The friar, knowing that Juliet is alive and hoping to bring the families to see the folly of their strife, at length steps forward with a conventional consolation expressed with unusual sharpness. Father, mother, groom, and nurse, as they kneel at the bedside, listen without remonstrance; usually their weeping has stopped before the end of the friar's speech.

**84-95** The formality of Capulet's reply expresses a bitter acceptance of Juliet's death. His last line can sound like recognition of his own impotence, although hardly of his own guilt as the friar hoped.

The friar again emphasizes guilt in his last pointed couplet: this will also remind the audience of earlier intimations of Fate, especially the words of the Chorus and of Romeo and Juliet. On his own account, the friar will be conscious chiefly of his

FRIAR Sir go you in; and madam go with him;
And go Sir Paris. Everyone prepare
To follow this fair corse unto her grave.
The heavens do lou'r° upon you for some ill;°
Move° them no more by crossing their high will.
*Exeunt, [casting rosemary on her and shutting the curtains.]*
[NURSE *and* MUSCIANS] *manent.*°

FIRST MUSICIAN Faith we may put up our pipes° and be gone.

NURSE Honest goodfellows, ah put up, put up!
For well you know this is a pitiful case.° [*Exit.*]

FIRST MUSICIAN Ay by my troth, the case may be amended.

*Enter* PETER.

PETER Musicians, O musicians, "Heart's ease,"° "Heart's ease:"! O, an you will have me live, play "Heart's ease"!

FIRST MUSICIAN Why "Heart's ease"?

PETER O musicians, because my heart itself plays "My heart is full." O play me some merry dump° to comfort me!

FIRST MUSICIAN Not a dump we: 'tis no time to play° now.

PETER You will not then?

FIRST MUSICIAN No.

PETER I will then give it you soundly.°

FIRST MUSICIAN What will you give us?

PETER No money on my faith, but the gleek.° I will give you the minstrel.°

FIRST MUSICIAN Then will I give you the serving creature.

PETER Then will I lay the serving creature's dagger on your pate. I will carry° no crotchets.° I'll *re* you, I'll *fa* you.° Do you note° me?

FIRST MUSICIAN An you *re* us and *fa* us, you note° us.

SECOND MUSICIAN Pray you put up your dagger, and put out° your wit.

machinations: full recognition of his own guilt and the operation of Fate on himself does not come until V.iii.153-4.

The departure of the Capulets and Paris will take some time; as they silently take leave of Juliet's supposed corpse, each will express his or her own silent reaction.

frown on, threaten  on account of some sin
anger

remain (L.)

"shut up"/pack up our instruments

situation/instrument case

**95-99** The nurse's words before her exit are the last she speaks in the play; she probably waits a moment and then leaves weeping. The pun on "case" is often said as if it is an attempt to conceal her sorrow and, possibly, her sense of guilt.

(a popular tune)

a sad tune

have a game/make music

thoroughly/with a noise

jeer

I will show you up as a hired musician

put up with  whims/notes
sound the notes (puns: "ray" = befoul; "fay" = clean out)  understand

set down in music

exert

**100-36** Peter probably enters weeping profusely, for this was a traditional fool's *entré*. Perhaps he stops wailing to make his request and then bursts out again at the end of line 104.

Shakespeare has used Peter and the musicians to give some relief between pathetic and intense scenes and the presentation of Romeo in exile at the start of Act V. During this talk, in Elizabethan performances, the bed, clothing, and other properties could be removed from the stage. At the same time, the tomb could be set up within the curtained area at the back of the stage so that it is ready in good time for V.iii and without danger of disturbing V.i with backstage noise. In twentieth-century theatres which can change a stage setting rapidly and noiselessly, this episode with the musicians is frequently cut altogether and the music alone used to make a suitable and swifter transition to the next scene

After comic weeping, there are the beginnings of a fight and then a "wit" combat. In the latter, Peter again speaks of "grief" but soon forgets his sorrow in the pleasures of contest and fooling. He leaves the stage very pleased with himself; he may go out singing or with another sudden flood of sobbing.

The third musician has been given a delayed entry into the talk and so gains special attention. With his one line (131), he can sound truly perplexed or truly sorrowful; or he can be so scornful or uninterested that he accentuates the triviality of the others.

PETER Then have at° you with my wit! I will dry-beat° you with an iron° wit, and put up my iron dagger. Answer me like men.

"When griping grief the heart doth wound,
And doleful dumps° the mind oppress,
Then music with her silver sound°—"

Why "silver sound"? Why "music with her silver sound"? What say you Simon Catling?°

FIRST MUSICIAN Marry sir, because silver hath a sweet sound.

PETER Pretty! What say you Hugh Rebeck?°

SECOND MUSICIAN I say "silver sound" because musicians sound for silver.

PETER Pretty too! What say you James Soundpost?°

THIRD MUSICIAN Faith I know not what to say.

PETER O I cry you mercy,° you are the singer. I will say for you. It is "music with her silver sound" because musicians have no gold for sounding.°

"Then music with her silver sound
With speedy help doth lend redress." *Exit.*

FIRST MUSICIAN What a pestilent knave is this same!

SECOND MUSICIAN Hang him, Jack!° Come, we'll in here, tarry for the mourners, and stay° dinner. *Exit [with others.]*

attack beat soundly
merciless

sorrows
(Apollo, god of song, had a lyre with silver strings)

cat gut (lute string)

three-stringed fiddle

part of inner structure of a violin

beg your pardon

in payment for music/to jingle

knave
wait for

**137-39** The brief comments of the musicians on their exits serve as a return to the basic narrative interest and to the customary accommodations of ordinary, non-tragic living: so, after its wailing, "confusions," moralizing, and crossed purposes, the scene finishes quietly.

# ACT V

Scene i *Enter* Romeo.

Romeo If I may trust the flattering truth of sleep,
My dreams presage some joyful news at hand.
My bosom's lord° sits lightly in his throne,°
And all this day an unaccustomed spirit
Lifts me above the ground with cheerful thoughts.
I dreamt my lady came and found me dead—
Strange dream that gives a dead man leave to think—
And breathed such life with kisses in my lips
That I revived and was an emperor.
Ah me, how sweet is love itself possessed,
When but love's shadows° are so rich in joy!

*Enter* Romeo*'s man* Balthasar, [*booted.*]

News from Verona! How now, Balthasar,
Dost thou not bring me letters from the friar?
How doth my lady? Is my father well?
How fares my Juliet? That I ask again,
For nothing can be ill if she be well.

Balthasar Then she is well,° and nothing can be ill.
Her body sleeps in Capel's monument,°
And her immortal part with angels lives.
I saw her laid low in her kindred's vault,
And presently° took post° to tell it you.
O pardon me, for bringing these ill news,
Since you did leave it for my office° sir.

Romeo Is it e'en so? Then I defy° you, stars!
Thou knowest my lodging: get me ink and paper,

i.e., Cupid i.e., Romeo's heart

phantoms

i.e., in heaven

tomb

immediately post horse

duty

challenge, reject

ACT V. Scene i

**1-11** Romeo, elated and nervous, cannot reconcile his "cheerful thoughts" with an earlier and contrary mistrust: as soon as he has spoken of the height of this unreal pleasure, he stops and sighs "Ah me." Interpreted in this way, the whole soliloquy depends on its opening "If" and "Strange" of line 7 implies untrustworthiness. In this restless mood, he sees Balthasar as soon as he enters and, probably, goes to him at once.

However, some Romeos speak these lines as if the thoughts of being "dead" far outweigh the "presage" of joyful news and only Balthasar's entry gives any vitality to the banished lover.

**12-23** In contrast to Romeo's eagerness to hear what he has to say, Balthasar dreads giving his news; he stands still and says nothing to all the questions. Line 16 suggests that Romeo senses disaster before Balthasar brings himself to speak his first careful and terrible line.

Romeo, stunned, remains silent, so that Balthasar continues and precisely tells the news that had been implicit in his first line. By the end of line 21, Balthasar sees that his task is over: probably, Romeo has moved away or has hidden his face in his hands.

**24-34** Romeo breaks his silence with one highly charged line. Laurence Olivier, at the Old Vic, London, said it "tonelessly" as if at the end of all

And hire post horses; I will hence tonight.

BALTHASAR I do beseech you sir, have patience;
Your looks are pale and wild, and do import°
Some misadventure.°

ROMEO Tush, thou art deceived.
Leave me, and do the thing I bid thee do.
Hast thou no letters to me from the friar?

BALTHASAR No, my good lord.

ROMEO No matter. Get thee gone;
And hire those horses. I'll be with thee straight.°
*Exit* [BALTHASAR.]
Well, Juliet, I will lie with thee tonight.
Let's see for means. O mischief,° thou art swift
To enter in the thoughts of desperate men!
I do remember an apothecary—
And hereabouts 'a° dwells—which late I noted
In tatt'red weeds,° with overwhelming° brows,
Culling of simples.° Meager were his looks;
Sharp misery had worn him to the bones.
And in his needy shop a tortoise hung,
An alligator stuffed, and other skins
Of ill-shaped fishes; and about his shelves
A beggarly account° of empty boxes,
Green earthen pots, bladders, and musty seeds,
Remnants of packthread, and old cakes of roses°
Were thinly scattered, to make up a show.
Noting this penury, to myself I said,
"An if a man did need a poison now—
Whose sale is present death° in Mantua—
Here lives a caitiff° wretch would sell it him."
O this same thought did but forerun° my need,
And this same needy man must sell it me.
As I remember, this would be the house.
Being holiday, the beggar's shop is shut.
What ho, apothecary!

[*Enter* APOTHECARY.]

portend
bad fortune

immediately

wickedness

he
clothes overhanging*
sorting out medicinal herbs

wretched collection

pressed rose petals

immediate death is the penalty for its sale
base
anticipate

resource of spirit, and this was "very moving" (*Sunday Times*, 20 Nov., 1935). Other actors take the first half of the line rapidly or vigorously and then, with its second half, becoming determined, angry, rash, or appalled. Sometimes the entire line may sound ineffectual.

Romeo has recognized a concatenation of events and the very next moment, in a flash, determines to do what seems to him inevitable. He looks "pale and wild" (l. 28), active with inner desperation and certainty. At line 29, he pretends to take the news lightly and perhaps smiles; but short phrases, the sudden thought of the friar and its more rapid dismissal, and his insistence on speed, all continue to express his now determined purpose. He sends his servant away brusquely, for he needs to be alone. Romeo then addresses Juliet, expressing in one line (34) the longing and love that has lain still deeper within him than the new sense of doom and desperation or his memory of a "flattering" dream: this is a still, quiet moment.

**35-57** Romeo breaks off his thoughts of Juliet and begins to plan his own death. He speaks quickly until his memory of the apothecary's poverty and outlandishness seems to take over in his mind. Alan Badel, at the Old Vic Theatre, London, spoke "as a man in a fever"; the tortoise and the alligator seemed "as things of nightmare" (*The Lady*, 2 Dec., 1952).

Lines 53-4 suggest that Romeo sees all that he is now doing as preordained and unalterable, even though he has chosen to defy the stars (see line 24); he is not at all surprized when he finds that he happens to be outside the Apothecary's house. He probably looks dazed but also purposeful; and he seems to know that the apothecary will answer at once, as if he has been waiting for him.

APOTHECARY Who calls so loud?

ROMEO Come hither man. I see that thou art poor.
Hold, there is forty ducats.° Let me have
A dram of poison, such soon-speeding gear°
As will disperse itself through all the veins,
That the life-weary taker may fall dead
And that the trunk° may be discharged of breath
As violently as hasty powder° fired
Doth hurry from the fatal cannon's womb.

APOTHECARY Such mortal° drugs I have; but Mantua's law
Is death to any he that utters° them.

ROMEO Art thou so bare and full of wretchedness,
And fearest to die? Famine is in thy cheeks,
Need and oppression starveth in thy eyes,°
Contempt and beggary hangs upon thy back.°
The world is not thy friend, nor the world's law;
The world affords no law to make thee rich;
Then be not poor, but break it° and take this.

APOTHECARY My poverty, but not my will consents.

ROMEO I pay thy poverty and not thy will.

APOTHECARY Put this in any liquid thing you will
And drink it off, and, if you had the strength
Of twenty men, it would dispatch you straight.°

ROMEO There is thy gold°—worse poison to men's souls,
Doing more murders in this loathsome world,
Than these poor compounds that thou mayst not sell.
I sell thee poison; thou hast sold me none.
Farewell. Buy food and get thyself in flesh.
Come, cordial° and not poison, go with me
To Juliet's grave; for there must I use thee. *Exeunt.*

gold coins
quick-working stuff

body
gunpowder

deadly
dispenses

your eyes show you are dying from need and distress
your clothes reveal your despised poverty

i.e., the law

immediately

(used as medicinal *cordial*)

medicine (tonic for the heart)

**68-86** The apothecary can look like Death himself (as depicted in medieval and early Renaisance art, especially in the "Dance of Death" which showed him summoning mortals to leave their lives). If so, his warning about the dangers of selling poison is a way of enticing Romeo into full commitment to the act of suicide. He has the poison ready before it is asked for. His silent exit marks the completion of the pact and Death's assurance that he will feed on Romeo (l. 79). He may well laugh when he is told to "get" himself in "flesh" (l. 84).

Alternatively and more simply, the apothecary can be a poor tradesman who is genuinely afraid of Romeo's desperate boldness, holding back (see line 58) and saying as little as possible. He will hurry offstage (after l. 75) to fetch the poison and will whisper his instructions. He takes the gold and leaves inconspicuously—although he may be held back for a moment as Romeo surprises him by wishing him well (l. 84).

The last two lines of the scene are a soliloquy, in which Romeo again thinks of Juliet: "cordial" suggests that he feels restored to full life, now that he knows he is ready for death.

Scene ii *Enter* FRIAR JOHN.

FRIAR JOHN Holy Franciscan friar! Brother ho!

*Enter* FRIAR LAWRENCE.

FRIAR LAWRENCE This same should be the voice of Friar John.
Welcome from Mantua. What says Romeo?
Or if his mind be writ, give me his letter.

FRIAR JOHN Going to find a barefoot brother° out,
One of our order, to associate° me
Here in this city visiting the sick,
And finding him, the searchers° of the town,
Suspecting that we both were in a house
Where the infectious pestilence did reign,
Sealed up the doors,° and would not let us forth,
So that my speed to Mantua there was stayed.

FRIAR LAWRENCE Who bare my letter then to Romeo?

FRIAR JOHN I could not send it—here it is again—
Nor get a messenger to bring it thee,
So fearful were they of infection.

FRIAR LAWRENCE Unhappy fortune! By my brotherhood,°
The letter was not nice,° but full of charge,°
Of dear import;° and the neglecting it
May do much danger.° Friar John, go hence;
Get me an iron crow° and bring it straight
Unto my cell.

FRIAR JOHN Brother I'll go and bring it thee. *Exit.*

FRIAR LAWRENCE Now must I to the monument alone.
Within this three hours will fair Juliet wake.
She will beshrew° me much that Romeo
Hath had no notice of these accidents.°
But I will write again to Mantua,

Franciscan friar
accompany

health officers

i.e., to enforce quarantine

religious order
trivial weighty matters
utmost importance
harm
crowbar

reprove
happenings

## Scene ii

**1-22** The two friars look alike by reason of the habits they wear: Lawrence's question about Romeo will identify him and awaken the audience's curiosity. Disclosure is held back by the complicated syntax of Friar John's long reply (ll. 5-12); it is usually spoken with pedantic care, slowly and precisely. As he offers the letter to the momentarily speechless Lawrence (l. 14-6), the audience understands the confusion of purposes that Lawrence briefly recognizes and blames upon "fortune." At once, orders are issued and both become alert in the emergency: thoughts and words are simple, without imagery.

**23-29** Left alone Friar Lawrence is still concerned with immediate action; only the last line touches, briefly and comprehensively, on the full disaster as he sees it.

The whole of this lightly written scene gives an impression of small men hurrying about on the

And keep her at my cell till Romeo come—
Poor living corse, closed in a dead man's tomb! *Exit.*

Scene iii *Enter* County Paris *and his* Page, [*with flowers and sweet° water.*]

Paris Give me thy torch boy. Hence, and stand aloof.
Yet put it out, for I would not be seen.
Under yond yew trees lay thee all along,°
Holding thy ear close to the hollow° ground,
So shall no foot upon the churchyard tread—
Being loose, unfirm, with digging up of graves—
But thou shalt hear it. Whistle then to me,
As signal that thou hearest something approach.
Give me those flowers. Do as I bid thee, go.

Page [*Aside.*] I am almost afraid to stand° alone
Here in the churchyard; yet I will adventure.° [*Retires.*]

Paris Sweet flower,° with flowers thy bridal bed I strew—
O woe, thy canopy is dust and stones!—
Which with sweet water nightly I will dew,
Or wanting° that, with tears distilled by moans.
The obsequies that I for thee will keep,°
Nightly shall be to strew thy grave and weep.

Page *whistles.*

The boy gives warning something doth approach.
What cursèd foot wanders this way tonight
To cross° my obsequies and true love's rite?
What, with a torch? Muffle° me, night, awhile. [*Retires.*]

*Enter* Romeo *and* Balthasar [*with a torch, a mattock, and a crow of iron.*]

Romeo Give me that mattock and the wrenching iron.
Hold, take this letter. Early in the morning

periphery of the drama; they talk urgently and act decisively, but the audience knows that they are ignorant of the full situation.

scented

Scene iii

**1-11** At mention of a tomb by the friar at the end of the preceding scene, a tomb is disclosed onstage. In Elizabethan times, it would have been revealed from behind curtains or pushed onto center-stage. Juliet lies on a catafalque, surrounded by an iron grill. Tybalt's body also lies within a central enclosure and other monuments and tombs should be visible or, at least, invoked by the dialogue at ll. 60-1.

full length

echoing

Attention is deflected from the scene-setting by two cloaked figures who enter at a distance, possibly on an upper level of the stage. Paris speaks in an urgent whisper and in sufficient detail to ensure that his page (and the audience) understands. Especially when the torch is put out (see l. 2), they will move with extreme caution, unsure of their footing in the dark, "unfirm" graveyard.

stay

risk it

i.e., Juliet

The page reacts silently until Paris leaves him and then his frightened aside (ll. 10-1) still further heightens tension and gives Paris the opportunity to leave the upper stage and reappear below without breaking the build-up of tension.

lacking

observe regularly

**12-21** The formal and rhymed verses hold attention as they are spoken quietly and reverently; flowers are placed by Juliet's body and holy water is sprinkled. These rites probably continue wordlessly until silence is broken by a warning whistle. Reactions are immediate and Paris hides as footsteps come closer.

prevent

hide

**22-44** Romeo enters as Paris had done, only he keeps a torch lighted and carries iron tools, not flowers. Also he speaks more decisively, with controlled

See thou deliver it to my lord and father.
Give me the light. Upon thy life I charge thee,
Whate'er thou hearest or seest, stand all aloof,
And do not interrupt me in my course.°
Why I descend into this bed of death
Is partly to behold my lady's face,
But chiefly to take thence from her dead finger
A precious ring—a ring that I must use
In dear° employment.° Therefore hence, be gone.
But if thou, jealous,° dost return to pry
In what I farther shall intend to do,
By heaven I will tear thee joint by joint,
And strew this hungry° churchyard with thy limbs.
The time and my intents are savage-wild,
More fierce and more inexorable far
Than empty tigers or the roaring sea.

BALTHASAR I will be gone sir, and not trouble ye.

ROMEO So shalt thou show me friendship. Take thou that:°
Live, and be prosperous; and farewell, good fellow.

BALTHASAR [*Aside.*] For all this same, I'll hide me hereabout.
His looks I fear, and his intents I doubt.° [*Retires.*]

ROMEO Thou detestable maw,° thou womb of death,
Gorged with the dearest morsel° of the earth,
Thus I enforce thy rotten jaws to open,
And in despite° I'll cram thee with more food.
[ROMEO *opens the tomb.*]

PARIS This is that banished haughty Montague,
That murd'red my love's cousin—with which grief
It is supposed the fair creature died—
And here is come to do some villainous shame
To the dead bodies. I will apprehend him.
Stop thy unhallowed toil, vile Montague!
Can vengeance be pursued further than death?
Condemnèd villain, I do apprehend° thee.
Obey and go with me, for thou must die.

ROMEO I must indeed; and therefore came I hither.
Good gentle youth, tempt not a desp'rate man.

energy; he gives a strange, two-stage explanation for his actions (ll. 28-32). Having ordered his page away, he further warns, with an oath, that he will personally exact a terrible punishment on Balthasar should he "return to pry" (ll. 33-6). Even this does not satisfy Romeo; contradicting his earlier excuses for entering the tomb, he says that his intentions are "savage-wild" and inexorably destructive.

what I am doing

Once Balthasar has assured him of obedience, Romeo speaks of friendship in something more like his earlier manner, but briefly and dismissively (ll. 41-2). He probably leaves the upper level of the stage to reappear below as Balthasar speaks aside to voice an uncertainty the audience will well understand.

important/loving business

suspicious

i.e., ready to swallow bodies

i.e., money

suspect

stomach

i.e., Juliet

to spite you

**45-48** Romeo pauses when he sees the tomb and places his torch aside. The contrast with Paris's obsequies is marked: his words are agressively phrased, his images are physical and grotesque. With sounds of iron on iron, Romeo struggles to gain entry, speaking as if he needs to wrestle with the huge and horrible presence of a personified Death. The actor has to make a crucial choice here: Romeo can be so obsessed that he seems on the verge of breakdown or madness; or he can be so resolute and controlled that he is like a dangerous terrorist; or he can act like the inhuman instrument of some avenging Fate. His last words here must, however, show that his main intention is to commit suicide (l. 48).

**49-57** Paris speaks aside urgently, outraged by what he sees. At line 54, he draws his sword and comes out of hiding to confront Romeo; his voice is harsh and tense.

arrest

**58** Romeo answers with a doomed acceptance of death; he makes no attempt to escape.

**59-73** Paris can say nothing as Romeo urges his

Fly hence and leave me. Think upon these gone;
Let them affright thee. I beseech thee youth,
Put not another sin upon my head
By urging me to fury O be gone!
By heaven, I love thee better than myself,
For I come hither armed against myself.
Stay not, be gone. Live, and hereafter say,
A madman's mercy bid thee run away.

PARIS I do defy thy conjurations,°
And apprehend thee for a felon here.

ROMEO Wilt thou provoke me? Then have at thee boy!

[*They fight.*]

PAGE O Lord, they fight! I will go call the watch.

[*Exit.* PARIS *falls.*]

PARIS O I am slain! If thou be merciful,
Open the tomb, lay me with Juliet. [*Dies.*]

ROMEO In faith I will. Let me peruse this face.
Mercutio's kinsman, noble County Paris!
What said my man, when my betossèd soul
Did not attend° him as we rode? I think
He told me Paris should have married Juliet.
Said he not so, or did I dream it so?
Or am I mad, hearing him talk of Juliet,
To think it was so? O give me thy hand,
One writ with me in sour misfortune's book!
I'll bury thee in a triumphant grave.
A grave? O no! A lantern,° slaught'red youth,
For here lies Juliet, and her beauty makes
This vault a feasting° presence° full of light.
Death,° lie thou there, by a dead man interred.

[*Lays him in the tomb.*]

How oft when men are at the point of death
Have they been merry, which their keepers° call
A lightning° before death. O how may I
Call this a lightning? O my love, my wife,
Death that hath sucked the honey of thy breath,
Hath had no power yet upon thy beauty.

unknown assailant to go, trying successively to warn, frighten, and explain.

At line 69, Paris moves toward Romeo and at once they fight in near darkness. The struggle is suddenly over as Paris falls, his last words clearly heard in the following silence. He dies quickly, using what strength remains to urge Romeo to place him beside Juliet.

solemn entreaties/evil spells

**74-83** In the stillness after death, Romeo kneels by the side of Paris and stays there, trying to understand, to disentangle from his own fearful fantasies the reality he now faces. He wonders if he is going "mad" (l. 80) and then impulsively accepts a fellowship in misfortune, transcending feud and rivalry. Line 82 can be spoken in calm acceptance or in bitter acknowledgment of mutual helplessness.

listen to

**84-91** For a moment, Romeo's sense of Juliet's beauty transforms his thoughts. As he returns to his task and drags Paris's corpse across the stage, a bitter joke shows his keen awareness of an inescapable doom (l. 87). The following lines suggest that Romeo may force a laugh at his own jest and then, seeing Juliet, stop himself from doing so.

superstructure with windows all around

festive throne room

i.e., the body of Paris

**91-115** Romeo cries out in the heartfelt, simple words, "love" and "wife." As he gazes on her, his fierce desperation is forgotten and so is any thought that he is going mad: he goes to her side and sees that she is glowing with life. He speaks to express an overpowering sense of reverence and the sheer pleasure her beauty gives.

nurses, jailers

lightening of spirit/illumination

He looks away, probably to realize better what is happening, and so sees Tybalt's corpse: he is reminded of his own fate and then of his need for for-

Thou art not conquered: Beauty's ensign° yet
Is crimson in thy lips and in thy cheeks,
And Death's pale flag is not advancèd° there.
Tybalt, liest thou there in thy bloody sheet?
O what more favor° can I do to thee
Than with that hand that cut thy youth in twain
To sunder his that was thine enemy?°
Forgive me, cousin. Ah, dear Juliet,
Why art thou yet so fair? Shall I believe
That unsubstantial° Death is amorous,
And that the lean abhorred monster keeps
Thee here in dark to be his paramour?°
For fear of that I still° will stay with thee
And never from this palace of dim night
Depart again. Here, here will I remain
With worms that are thy chambermaids. O here
Will I set up my everlasting rest,°
And shake the yoke of inauspicious stars
From this world-wearied flesh. Eyes look your last!
Arms take your last embrace! And lips, O you
The doors of breath, seal with a righteous kiss
A dateless° bargain to engrossing° death!
Come bitter conduct, come unsavory guide;
Thou desperate pilot, now at once run on
The dashing rocks thy seasick weary bark!°
Here's to my love! [*Drinks.*] O true° apothecary,
Thy drugs are quick!° Thus with a kiss I die. [*Falls.*]

*Enter* FRIAR LAWRENCE, *with a lantern, crow, and spade.*

FRIAR LAWRENCE Saint Francis be my speed!° How oft tonight
Have my old feet stumbled° at graves! Who's there?

BALTHASAR Here's one, a friend, and one that knows you well.

FRIAR LAWRENCE Bliss be upon you! Tell me, good my friend,
What torch is yond that vainly° lends his light
To grubs and eyeless skulls? As I discern,
It burneth in the Capel's monument.

BALTHASAR It doth so, holy sir; and there's my master,
One that you love.

sign/banner

raised up

good turn/mark of honor

to kill your killer (Romeo)

without a body*

mistress

always

stake my eternal all/build my hopes of immortal peace

endless possession-taking/monopolizing

i.e., Romeo's body

promising truly/true-working

speedy/alive/life-giving

protector

(supposedly an ill omen)

uselessly

giveness. On this, he turns to Juliet again (l. 101), and again speaks to her, intimately, as if she were alive. But now this only reminds him of death and suggests more vividly the horror of the grave (ll. 105-9). With harsh punning and vigorous imagery (ll. 110-2), he prepares to die. Some Romeos embrace and kiss Juliet at lines 112-15; others wait until after taking the poison (see line 120) to enact what these lines describe.

The whole of Romeo's last speech has sustained energy of thought and feeling. Questions, comments, vows, and exclamations reveal the waves of emotions—of love, despair, hope, pain—that course through him. Images throng into his mind: luminous, physical, military, royal; elemental images that seem to develop and change in his mind even as he speaks and to be impelled by instinctive tenderness and despair. The most constant element is a metrical control, which can suggest a stability or assurance, a homing instinct, underneath each changing expression of feeling. This impression is heightened during the later lines, for the audience if not for Romeo, because they echo earlier speeches and so seem to fulfill earlier intimations: V.i.62, 77-79, and 85, the "pilot" images of I.iv.106-13, II.ii.82-84, and III.i.118, and Juliet's drinking of the potion at IV.iii.58-59.

The audience knows that Juliet is not dead, as Romeo believes, and lines 92-6 and 101-5 are reminders, among all the passionate intensity, that he is deceived and his suicide unnecessary.

**116-20** With urgent vocal rhythms, Romeo takes out the apothecary's poison and pours it into a cup (see line 161). Only line 118 runs without break as its imagery expresses a sense of helplessness and violence. In half a line Romeo pledges his love—a brief moment of strong and simple feeling—and then, with rapid, punning acknowledgment of pain and wordplay on the Elizabethan use of die = "have sexual satisfaction," he embraces Juliet, kisses her, and, a moment later, is dead at her side.

In his last moments, Romeo acts singlemindedly: he may seem to be in a dream, already lost to the world; or he may be, as if miraculously, wholly in command and unhurried. Alternatively, the ending can be played desperately, with Romeo struggling to maintain control as he is terribly racked by pain, frustrated desire, and fear of life.

**121-39** After a moment's silence in which the audience realizes that Romeo is dead, the friar hurries on and encounters Balthasar at the entrance to the

FRIAR LAWRENCE Who is it?

BALTHASAR Romeo.

FRIAR LAWRENCE How long hath he been there?

BALTHASAR Full half an hour.

FRIAR LAWRENCE Go with me to the vault.

BALTHASAR I dare not, sir.
My master knows not but I am gone hence,
And fearfully did menace me with death
If I did stay to look on his intents.

FRIAR LAWRENCE Stay then; I'll go alone. Fear comes upon me:
O much I fear some ill unthrifty° thing.

BALTHASAR As I did sleep under this yew tree here,
I dreamt my master and another fought,
And that my master slew him.

FRIAR LAWRENCE Romeo!
Alack, alack, what blood is this which stains
The stony entrance of this sepulcher?
What mean these masterless° and gory swords
To lie discolored by this place of peace? [*Enters the tomb.*]
Romeo! O pale! Who else? What, Paris too?
And steeped in blood? Ah what an unkind° hour
Is guilty of this lamentable chance!
The lady stirs. [JULIET *rises.*]

JULIET O comfortable° Friar, where is my lord?
I do remember well where I should be,
And there I am. Where is my Romeo?

FRIAR LAWRENCE I hear some noise. Lady, come from that nest
Of death, contagion, and unnatural sleep.
A greater power than we can contradict
Hath thwarted our intents. Come, come away.
Thy husband in thy bosom there lies dead;
And Paris too. Come, I'll dispose of° thee
Among a sisterhood of holy nuns.
Stay not to question, for the watch° is coming.
Come, go good Juliet: I dare no longer stay. *Exit.*

tomb. His questions are urgent, but he hesitates before going down, fearing some disaster (ll. 135-6). When Balthasar suggests that Romeo has already killed someone, the friar starts immediately to go down to the tomb.

harmful, wasteful

**140-59** The friar cries out as he discovers each sign of disaster, but then Juliet moves and an incomplete verse-line (147) suggests that he goes to her and waits for her to speak. He does not, however, answer her questions, which show him the terrible consequences of what he has brought about (ll. 148, 150). All is very quiet, so that the friar hears a slight noise offstage. He is afraid, and his first instinct is to leave at once with Juliet, not yet telling her that Romeo is dead. He does not give this information until after he has blamed the overpowering influence of fate and again urged her to leave. Juliet reacts quite differently: even when the Friar has confessed that her husband is dead, she continues to neither move nor speak. The sounds of the watch coming nearer and the Friar's frightened departure do not affect her either.

abandoned by their owners

unnatural

comforting

From line 155 onwards, the friar begins to panic so much that, thinking of his own safety, he leaves Juliet with no one to help her in a most appalling situation for which he must count himself responisble. For the actor, if he does not want to lose all the audience's sympathy, the best course is to play this moment as if crazed out of his mind, or as if compelled by the fate which he acknowledges to be greater than himself (see ll. 153-4). Either task is difficult and the actor may well hope that the audience will be so concerned for Juliet that the friar may escape without attracting too much attention.

place

watchmen

JULIET Go, get thee hence, for I will not away.
What's here? A cup, closed° in my true love's hand?
Poison, I see, hath been his timeless° end.
O churl,° drunk all, and left no friendly drop
To help me after? I will kiss thy lips:
Haply some poison yet doth hang on them
To make die with a restorative.° [*Kisses him.*]
Thy lips are warm!

CHIEF WATCHMAN [*Within.*] Lead, boy. Which way?

JULIET Yea, noise? Then I'll be brief. O happy° dagger,
[*Snatches Romeo's dagger.*]
This° is thy sheath! There rust, and let me die.
[*She stabs herself and falls.*]

*Enter* PARIS' PAGE *and* WATCH.

PAGE This is the place: there, where the torch doth burn.

CHIEF WATCHMAN The ground is bloody. Search about the churchyard.
Go some of you, whoe'er you find attach.°
[*Exeunt some of the* WATCH.]
Pitiful sight! Here lies the county slain;
And Juliet bleeding, warm, and newly dead,
Who here hath lain these two days burièd.
Go, tell the Prince. Run to the Capulets.
Raise up the Montagues. Some others search.
[*Exeunt others of the* WATCH.]
We see the ground° whereon these woes° do lie,
But the true ground° of all these piteous woes
We cannot without circumstance° descry.

*Enter* [*some of the* WATCH, *with*] ROMEO'S *Man*, BALTHASAR.

SECOND WATCHMAN Here's Romeo's man; we found him in the churchyard.

CHIEF WATCHMAN Hold him in safety, till the Prince come hither.

held

untimely

ill-mannered fellow

i.e., the kiss she gives

fortunately at hand / successful

i.e., her breast

arrest

earth woeful creatures*

reason

details

**160-67** In contrast with the friar's increasing agitation, Juliet's first words are assured. In the growing commotion, she has seen her husband dead and has passed beyond fear, anger, disbelief, sense of loss, or any other response except the need to be with him. As she kisses him she seems to recognize life (l. 167).

This short speech is perhaps the most astonishing in the whole role of Juliet. Into its first line, "uttered with no raised voice, uttered so slowly and lethally, into every syllable and sound of it, [Julia Marlowe as Juliet] put a finality more appalling than any vehemence could have been" (C. E. Russell, *Julia Marlowe* [1926], p. 238). In contrast with this, "Thy lips are warm" can have a simplicity that compels belief and expresses loving tenderness or, alternatively, a half-crazed imagination.

**168-70** As the sounds offstage become more discernible, Juliet sees the dagger, takes it, and with one thrust kills herself. Her rhythms are short and urgent; her words imply power, satisfaction, and fulfillment. As Romeo had done, she ends with "die," used punningly, as in much Elizabethan love poetry, of sexual satisfaction.

**171-87** The watch, armed, appear where Paris and Romeo had entered. They come and go, and search about the stage, as numerous orders are given. There will be a still moment when the bodies are discovered (ll. 174-75). When the prisoners are brought in, they will momentarily gain full attention: the friar is quite changed; he "trembles, sighs, and weeps," and is speechless.

Movement is probably on two levels of the stage and there will be considerable noise from weapons, hurrying feet, and cries.

*Enter* FRIAR LAWRENCE *and another* WATCHMAN.

THIRD WATCHMAN Here is a friar that trembles, sighs, and weeps.
We took this mattock and this spade from him
As he was coming from this churchyard's side.

CHIEF WATCHMAN A great suspicion: stay the friar too.

*Enter the* PRINCE [*and* ATTENDANTS.]

PRINCE What misadventure is so early up,
That calls our person from our morning rest?

*Enter* CAPULET, *and* LADY CAPULET, [*with others.*]

CAPULET What should it be, that they so shrieked abroad?

LADY CAPULET O the people in the street cry "Romeo,"
Some "Juliet," and some "Paris"; and all run
With open° outcry toward our monument.°

PRINCE What fear is this which startles in your ears?

CHIEF WATCHMAN Sovereign, here lies the County Paris slain;
And Romeo dead; and Juliet, dead before,
Warm and new killed.

PRINCE Search, seek, and know how this foul murder comes.

CHIEF WATCHMAN Here is a friar, and slaughtered Romeo's man,
With instruments upon them fit to open
These dead men's tombs.

CAPULET O heavens! O wife, look how our daughter bleeds!
This dagger hath mista'en,° for lo his house°
Is empty on the back of Montague,
And it missheathèd in my daughter's bosom.

LADY CAPULET O me, this sight of death is as a bell°
That warns° my old age to a sepulcher.

*Enter* MONTAGUE [*and others.*]

**188-98** The Prince and his attendants probably appear first on the upper level. As they go down to the main stage, the Capulets enter above. Lines 191-3 suggest that all this is accompanied by renewed and growing cries offstage.

The half-line 197 indicates that the Prince (and everyone else) is silent after he learns the news. Perhaps he crosses himself before giving the necessary orders. Capulet and his lady may now start to descend to the tomb.

public tomb

gone astray its sheath

**202-7** As Capulet reaches the tomb, he cries out and goes to the two dead bodies. His wife is rather more controlled and austere; by her own account she is less than thirty years old (see I.iii.70-4) but now she appears to age in a moment (see l. 207). Both are silent, perhaps comforting each other, as Montague is seen entering at the upper level.

funeral bell

summons

PRINCE Come, Montague; for thou art early up
To see thy son and heir more early down.°

MONTAGUE Alas my liege, my wife is dead tonight;
Grief of my son's exile hath stopped her breath.
What further woe conspires against mine age?

PRINCE Look and thou shalt see.

MONTAGUE O thou untaught, what manners is in this,
To press before thy father to a grave?

PRINCE Seal up the mouth of outrage° for a while,
Till we can clear these ambiguities,
And know their spring,° their head, their true descent;
And then will I be general° of your woes
And lead you even to death. Meantime forbear,
And let mischance be slave to patience.°
Bring forth the parties of suspicion.

FRIAR I am the greatest;° able to do least,°
Yet most suspected, as the time and place
Doth make against° me, of this direful murder.
And here I stand, both to impeach and purge,°
Myself condemnèd and myself excused.

PRINCE Then say at once what thou dost know in this.

FRIAR I will be brief, for my short date of breath°
Is not so long as is a tedious tale.
Romeo, there dead, was husband to that Juliet;
And she, there dead, that's Romeo's faithful wife.
I married them; and their stol'n marriage day
Was Tybalt's doomsday, whose untimely death
Banished the new-made bridegroom from this city;
For whom, and not for Tybalt, Juliet pined.
You, to remove that siege° of grief from her,
Betrothed, and would have married her perforce,
To County Paris. Then comes she to me,
And with wild looks bid me devise some mean
To rid her from this second marriage,
Or in my cell there would she kill herself.
Then gave I her, so tutored by my art,
A sleeping potion; which so took effect

on the ground (dead)

**208-22** Montague, followed by his household, goes to the opposite side of the tomb from the Capulets. It is enemy territory to him, but the feuding families say nothing to each other. The incomplete line 213 suggests that he weeps or falls silently to his knees beside his son's body before speaking again.

The Prince takes command at line 216, speaking first to the mourners and then to the officers of his guard who have entered with him.

cease these violent cries

source

take charge

let disaster submit to patience

most suspicious weakest (because old and a friar)

implicate

accuse and exonerate

**223-27** Before any official can respond, the friar speaks. His voice is broken by weeping (see line 184) and his confidence is gone (see lines 153-4); yet his antitheses indicate a keen desire that all should be known and attention be paid to what he says. Probably he speaks with a quiet intensity that accentuates the silence with which he is heard and the astonishment of all who now see him, broken and under arrest (compare line 270).

duration of life

**229-70** The friar's long speech tells the audience nothing it does not know. In performance it is often cut, but it is difficult to dispense with only a part of it; the easier way is to omit the speech entirely. However, when it is spoken in full, it becomes clear that much of its effect is in the reactions of the characters onstage and not in its exposition. Neither the families nor the Prince knew anything of what the friar now tells them. Lines 231 and 232, in particular, make huge demands upon the persons who have no words to say; almost certainly, the friar will have to pause as they cry out and weep. He continues with utter simplicity as his next words begin a re-examination of his own responsibility for what has happened, that is continued with equal directness at lines 243, 246, 254, 262, and 265. Especially toward the end, he also returns repeatedly to the other aspect of the disaster of which he is entirely sure, its ill-fatedness (see ll. 234, 251, 258, 261). By the end,

oppression

As I intended, for it wrought on her
The form° of death. Meantime I writ to Romeo,
That he should hither come as° this dire night
To help to take her from her borrowed grave,
Being the time the potion's force should cease.
But he which bore my letter, Friar John,
Was stayed by accident, and yesternight
Returned my letter back. Then all alone,
At the prefixèd° hour of her waking,
Came I to take her from her kindred's vault,
Meaning to keep her closely° at my cell
Till I conveniently could send to Romeo.
But when I came, some minute ere the time
Of her awakening, here untimely lay
The noble Paris and true Romeo dead.
She wakes; and I entreated her come forth
And bear° this work of heaven with patience;
But then a noise did scare me from the tomb,
And she, too desperate, would not go with me,
But, as it seems, did violence on herself.
All this I know, and to the marriage
Her nurse is privy;° and if aught in this
Miscarried by my fault, let my old life
Be sacrificed, some hour before his time,
Unto the rigor of severest law.

PRINCE We still° have known thee for a holy man.
Where's Romeo's man? What can he say in this?

BALTHASAR I brought my master news of Juliet's death;
And then in post° he came from Mantua
To this same place, to this same monument.
This letter he early bid me give his father,
And threat'ned me with death, going in the vault,
If I departed not and left him there.

PRINCE Give me the letter. I will look on it.
Where is the county's page that raised the watch?
Sirrah, what made° your master in this place?

PAGE He came with flowers to strew his lady's grave;
And bid me stand aloof, and so I did.

appearance
on

all his listeners are quiet and motionless, as if stunned by the events that have been recounted; the friar is exhausted and on his knees.

The Prince's comment at line 270 serves to reduce the tension that has built up, so that other examinations can procede. The friar may well weep at this; he has no words.

prearranged

secretly

endure

in the know

always

**271-95** The Prince now takes command. Balthasar and the page, under close guard, speak when directed; both may kneel after giving their evidence. There will be a pause during which the Prince reads the friar's letter before carefully summing up its evidence (ll. 286-90), but the tension holds, so that no one speaks in this interval.

haste

At line 291, all attention is focused, first on Capulet and then on Montague: the pointed word “enemies” will strike home so that their bare names are unavoidable summonses. When the Prince continues, he needs no argument but sharpens his message by ironic wordplay on "joys" and "love." Capulet and Montague now may be kneeling, speechless, with the other "parties of suspicion" (see line 222).

did

At this still moment, the Prince, standing centerstage as judge, implicates himself: he speaks of his own fault and his own loss. In this, Shakespeare

Anon comes one with light to ope the tomb;
And by and by° my master drew on him;
And then I ran away to call the watch.

PRINCE This letter doth make good the friar's words,
Their course of love, the tidings of her death;
And here he writes that he did buy a poison
Of a poor pothecary, and therewithal°
Came to this vault to die and lie with Juliet.
Where be these enemies? Capulet. Montague.
See what a scourge° is laid upon your hate,
That heaven finds means to kill your joys° with love.°
And I, for winking° at your discords too,
Have lost a brace of kinsmen. All are punished.

CAPULET O brother Montague, give me thy hand.
This° is my daughter's jointure,° for no more
Can I demand.

MONTAGUE But I can give thee more;
For I will raise her statue in pure gold,
That whiles Verona by that name is known,
There shall no figure at such rate be set°
As that of true and faithful Juliet.

CAPULET As rich shall Romeo's by his lady's lie—
Poor° sacrifices of our enmity!

PRINCE A glooming° peace this morning with it brings:
The sun for sorrow will not show his head.
Go hence, to have more talk of these sad things;
Some shall be pardoned, and some punishèd.
For never was a story of more woe
Than this of Juliet and her Romeo. [*Exeunt.*]

FINIS

immediately

effected a considerable dramatic innovation: rarely will a dramatist who has set up a judge in authority deliberately weaken that character's ability to stand aloof. The Prince's last three words make him equal to the other mourners and those who have admitted complicity in the disaster. The central focus of the drama is no longer the judge; it is the two corpses.

therewith

whip, chastisement
children/pleasure  their love/ your love for them
turning a blind eye

i.e., the hand of friendship
marriage settlement

**296-304** When all is known and the action seems to have run out of impetus, Capulet moves toward Montague. Solemnly, he breaks his long silence and the two fathers take hands in front of the two dead lovers—to them a wholly unprecedented event, a seeming impossibility. After line 304, with its acknowledgment of loss and the first use of "our" to indicate common feeling and responsibility, the two may stand supporting each other; or they may kneel, in keeping with the religious imagery, side by side facing the lovers. In either case, their eyes rest only on the tomb and there can be a considerable silence before the Prince speaks.

no effigy be valued so highly

grievous (wordplay on *rich*)

dark, threatening*

**305-10** The concluding speech of this tragedy is verbally simple except for the foreboding "glooming." Here is no acclamation as at the end of *Hamlet* or *Macbeth*. The bodies are left on stage (contrast *Othello*, where they are hidden from sight, or *Lear*, where they are borne offstage), and the tragedy ends with files of characters and supernumeraries passing slowly by the tomb and leaving the stage, all waiting for further knowledge and for punishment or pardon. In this silent procession, some may be weeping or crossing themselves in prayer; each person will express an individual involvement in the tragedy.

Probably the friar is the last to leave, or possibly the two fathers. In some productions, such as Zeffirelli's at the Old Vic, London, the nurse has been present at the tomb and makes the last exit. However the ending is managed, the focus is on human suffering and complicity during the departures from the stage and then shifts to the two dead lovers when only they are left.

# Textual Notes

*Romeo and Juliet* was first printed in an incomplete and inadequate version. The title page of this Quarto reads: "An Excellent conceited Tragedy of Romeo and Juliet. As it hath been often (with great applause) played publicly, by the right Honorable the Lord of Hunsdon his servants"; it is dated 1597. Recent scholarship has shown that this text probably represents an acting version shortened and simplified for playing on tour by someone other than Shakespeare. Jay L. Halio has argued that the alterations were in great part undertaken by the author himself (see *Shakespeare's "Romeo and Juliet"; Texts, Contexts, and Interpretation* (1995), pp. 123-50). In the same year, however, David Farely-Hills countered this view with evidence that to the present editor argues more convincingly for someone else being responsible although working from a manuscript in Shakespeare's hand ("The Bad Quarto of *Romeo and Juliet*", *Shakespeare Survey*, 49 (1995), pp.27-44). Some of this Quarto's stage directions read as reports of stage action when a fuller text was being performed.

In 1599 a second Quarto appeared from a different publisher and printer, "newly corrected, augmented, and amended": it was subtitled "The Most Excellent and Lamentable Tragedy." This "good" Quarto is the ultimate source of all later editions, including that of the 1623 Folio of Shakespeare's complete works. The printer worked from Shakespeare's own manuscript or a close transcript from it. Speech-prefixes for some characters vary according to dramatic context, and some stage directions clearly represent suggestions made by the author, rather than the precise notes of a book-keeper or prompter. There are signs that he had revised the play at some time after writing the manuscript that lay behind the shortened touring version published in 1597. Some duplications and confusions are best explained as Shakespeare's first thoughts remaining, side-by-side, with his corrections. It has been further argued that until III.iv the manuscript used by the printer was a fair copy and, thereafter, Shakespeare's "foul," or working papers.

Unfortunately, the second, "good" Quarto was not particularly well printed. Some errors are obvious, and the printer was short of full stops and so frequently omitted them or used commas or colons instead. Most significantly, the manuscript copy was supplemented by a copy of the First

Quarto. Between I.ii.53 and I.iii.35, the printer worked directly from the "bad" version—perhaps a leaf of the manuscript was missing—and elsewhere he referred to the Quarto sporadically, probably when the manuscript was unclear and the earlier Quarto not hopelessly corrupt.

The following collation lists all substantive changes made in this present edition from the text of the second Quarto. The reading of this edition is quoted first, in italics, followed by the rejected second Quarto reading, in roman type. Where the preferred reading is from the first Quarto, this is noted within square brackets. Act and scene divisions have no authority (both Quartos being printed without divisions) but follow traditional practice of earlier editors; they have not been collated, nor have they been printed within square brackets in the text, as are the added stage directions.

I.i. 24 *in sense* [Q1] sense 28 *comes two*[Q1] comes 67,S.D. *Citizens* Offi. 114 *drew* [Q1] drive 141 *his* is 147 *sun* same 171 *create* [Q1] created 173 *well-seeming* welseeing [Q1 best seeming] 186 *lovers'* louing [Q1 a louers] 191 *left* lost 196 *Bid a* [Q1] A; make [Q1] *makes* 212 *makes* make

I.ii. 15 *She is* Shees 32 *on* one 46 *One* [Q1] On 65 *Vitruvio* Utruuio 68 *and Livia* [Q1], Liuia 87 *fires* fier

I.iii. 67, 68 *honor* [Q1] houre 100 *make it* [Q1] make

I.iv. 7-8 [Q1; Q2 omits] 23 *Mercutio* Horatio 31 *quote* cote 39 *done* [Q1] dum 42 *Of* [Q1] Or; *your* you 45 *like* [Q1] lights 47 *five* fine 57 *atomies* ottamie [Q1 Atomi] 63 *film* Philome [Q1 filmes] 66 *maid* [Q1] man 72 *O'er* [Q1] On 113 *sail* [Q1] sute

I.v. 1, 5, 10 *First Servingman* Ser. 3 *Second Servingman* 1. 9 Third Servingman 2. 12 Fourth Servingman 3. 16 *Ah ha* [Q1] Ah 93 *ready* [Q1] did readie 140 *this...this* 'tis...'tis [Q1 this...that]

II.i. 6 *Mercutio* [Q1; Q2 before "Call"] 9 one [Q1] on 10 *pronounce* [Q1] prouaunt; *dove* [Q1] day 12 *heir* [Q1] her 38 *open-arse and* open, or [Q1open Et caetera,]

II.ii. 16 *do* [Q1] to; *eyes* [Q1] eye 31 *pacing* [Q1] puffing

41 *face...part* [Q1] face, O be some other name 42 *O...name* [Q2 at end of line 41; Q1 omits] 83 *washed* [Q1] washeth 99 *havior* [Q1] behauior 101 *more cunning* [Q1] coying 110 *circled* [Q1] circle 161 *than mine* then [Q1 as mine] 166 *sweet* Neece 185 *Romeo* Iu. [Ro., at line 186] 187 *Hence...* [Q2 repeats III.i.1-4 before this line]

II.iii. 2 *Check'ring* [Q1] Checking 3 *fleckèd* [Q1] fleckeld 22 *sometime's* [Q1] sometime 74 *ring yet* [Q1] yet ringing

II.iv. 18 *Cats,...you* [Q1] Cats 26 *fantasticoes* [Q1] phantacies 102 *made for* [Q1] made, 187 *Ah* A

II.v. 11 *three* there

II.vi. 27 *music's* musicke

III.i. 2 *are abroad* [Q1] abroad 86 *both your* both [Q1 your] 116 *Alive* [Q1] He gan 118 *eyed* [Q1] end 159 *agile* [Q1] aged 177 *Montague* Capulet 181 *hate's* [Q1] hearts 185 *I* [Q1] It

III.ii. 9 *By* and by 15 *grown* grow 21 *he* I 49 *shut* shot 51 *of my* my 60 *one* on 72 *Nurse* [Q1;Q2 before line 73] 76 *Dove-feathered* Rauenous dovefeathered 79 *damnèd* dimme

III.iii. S.D. *Friar* [Q1] Frier and Romeo 15 *Hence* [Q1] Here 39 *sin* sin./This may flyes do, when I from this must flie,/And sayest thou yet, that exile is not death? 52 *Thou* [Q1] Then 61 *madmen* [Q1] mad man 80, S.D. *Enter Nurse* after line 78 116 *lives* [Q1] lies 142 *misbehaved* [Q1] mishaued 143 *pout'st upon* puts up[Q1 frownst upon] 167 *disguised* disguise

III.v. 13 *exhales* [Q1] exhale 36, S.D. *Nurse* Madame and Nurse 83 *pardon him* padon 140 *gives* giue 182 *trained* [Q1] liand

IV.i. 7 *talked* [Q1] talk 72 *slay* [Q1] stay 83 *chapless* [Q1] chapels 85 *his shroud* his 98 *breath* [Q1] breast 100 *wanny* many 110 *bier* Beere,/Be borne to buriall in thy kindreds graue

IV.iv. 21 *faith* father

IV.v. 41 *long* [Q1] loue 81 *In all* [Q1] And in 82 *fond* some 98, S.D. *Exit* Exit omnes [at line 99] 119 *PETER* [after "my wit"] 121 *grief* [Q1] griefes 122 *And...oppress* [Q1; Q2 omits]

V.i. 15 *fares my* [Q1] doth my Lady 24 *defy* [Q1] denie 33, S.D. [after "Lord," line 32] 76 *pay* [Q1] pray

V.iii. 3. *yew* [Q1] young 21, S.D. *BALTHASAR* [Q1] PETER 68 *conjurations* [Q1] commiration 71 *PAGE* [Q2 omits; Q1 Boy] 102 *Shall I believe/That* I will beleue/Shall I belieue that 107 *palace* pallat 108 *again. Here* againe, come lye thou in my arme,/Heer's to thy helth, where ere thou tumblest in./O true Appothecarie!/Thy drugs are quick. Thus with a kiss a die./Depart againe, here 137 *yew* yong 170, S.D. [Q1 after line 167] 190 *shrieked* shrike 199 *slaughtered* Slaughter 201 [Q2 repeats "Enter Capulet and Wife"] 209 *more early* [Q1] now earling

John Russell Brown has been a fellow of the Shakespeare Institute, Stratford upon Avon, the first head of the Dept of Drama and Theatre Arts at the Dept of Drama in Birmingham (UK) and an Associate Director for the Royal National Theatre.

In the US he has taught at Columbia University and the University of Michigan. He has written about plays, acting and theatre and directed many plays in the UK and the US. Among his books that are available through Applause are: *Free Shakespeare*, *Shakespeare's Plays in Performance* and *Shakescenes.* His new book *Shakespeare: The Tragedies* will be published in February 2001.

# SHAKESPEARE'S PLAYS IN PERFORMANCE by John Russell Brown

In this volume, John Russell Brown snatches Shakespeare from the clutches of dusty academics and thrusts him centerstage where he belongs—in performance.

Brown's thorough analysis of the theatrical experience of Shakespeare forcibly demonstrates how the text is brought to life: awakened, colored, emphasized, and extended by actors and audiences, designers and directors.

"A knowledge of what precisely can and should happen when a play is performed is, for me, the essential first step towards an understanding of Shakespeare."
*—from the Introduction by John Russell Brown*

**paper•ISBN 1-55783-136-X•**